# An Apple a Day

## Keeps the Blues Away

Apples are far more than knock-your-socks-off delicious right off the tree. They make for great ingredients in lots of recipes.

HERE ARE SOME OF THOSE RECIPES

If you do eat 'em right off the tree, don't do like my uncle....go ahead and pick 'em first.

# Table of Contents

Some of the recipes in this book allude to preservation by canning. The instructions in this book are simply meant as guides for the reader.

These guides are not to be interpreted as detailed instructions, and the writer or publisher does not assume liability for damage or loss resulting from the use of these guides. Preservation by canning is a practice that requires exact care. The reader must consult other sources for safe ways to preserve by canning.

Dedicated to Joe Seaver

# Appetizers and Beverages

# Echinacea Ruby Apple Juice

1 medium beet (scrubbed & cut into medium pieces)
1 Granny Smith apple (halved, seeded & cut into medium pieces)
2 T. freshly squeezed lime juice
½ C. sparkling water (chilled) (plus more to taste)
½ tsp. echinacea-goldenseal extract

Place beet in a juice extractor and process, extracting all juice. Transfer juice to a pitcher. Place apple in juice extractor and process, extracting all juice. Transfer juice to the sparkling water. Stir well. Add ¼ tsp. echinacea extract to each of two small glasses. Divide juice between glasses and serve. Add more sparkling water and ice, if desired.

# Hot Mulled Cider

2 qt. apple cider
1 tsp. grated orange rind
1/2 tsp. whole allspice
1/4 tsp. mace
1/2 tsp. ground coriander
1 tsp. whole cloves
1 T. cinnamon candy (Red Hots)
Orange slices or whole cinnamon sticks

Bring all ingredients, except orange slices/cinnamon sticks, to boil in large kettle. Reduce heat and simmer for 30 minutes. Strain and serve hot with orange slices or whole cinnamon sticks. Yield: 8 (1-cup) servings.

# Dipped Fruit

1 (7 oz.) jar marshmallow creme
6 oz. light cream cheese
2 apples
32 strawberries

1. Combine marshmallow creme and cream cheese and blend with mixer until well combined.
2. Slice each apple into 16 pieces.
3. Place dip in serving bowl and arrange apples and strawberries on a plate with dip.

**Yield: 16 servings**

# Apple 'n Pineapple Slush

1 (46 oz.) can pineapple
  juice
1 (46 oz.) can apple juice

1 (2-liter) btl. Diet Sprite or
  Diet 7-Up
Orange slices & long-
  stemmed cherries (optional)

1. In a large container, combine juices. Freeze.
2. Remove from freezer about 3 hours before serving. If still frozen, break up. Should be slush consistency.
3. Add Diet Sprite or Diet 7-Up and mix.
4. Garnish with orange slices and long-stemmed cherries.

**Yield: 26**

# Christmas Cider

6 sticks cinnamon
16 cloves, cut up
1 tsp. whole allspice
2 orange slices

6 C. apple juice or cider
2 C. cranberry juice cocktail
4 C. sugar

Put cinnamon, cloves and allspice in bag. Simmer all ten minutes. Take out bag and oranges. Add 1 C. rum (optional). Pour over round peppermint candy in a cup and serve hot.

# Cider Sherbet Pick Ya' Up

2 qts. apple juice or cider
1 qt. lemon sherbet
Sprigs of mint

1 (10 oz.) bottle lemon-lime
carbonated beverage

Pour the chilled apple juice over the sherbet which has been spooned into punch bowl. Just before serving, pour the carbonated beverage in gently. Garnish with sprigs of mint. Makes 12 servings.

# Apple Wine Punch

½ C. sugar
½ C. water
1 lemon (thinly sliced)
1 orange (thinly sliced)
8 whole cloves

1 stick cinnamon
½ C. orange juice
2 C. apple juice or cider
2 C. Burgundy or claret wine

Mix together sugar, water, lemon and orange slices, cloves and cinnamon. Bring to a boil over low heat and simmer 5 minutes. Add the orange and apple juices and reheat. Add the wine and reheat but do not boil. Strain and serve at once. If you serve from a punch bowl, float the lemon and orange slices in the punch. Makes about 6 cups.

# Apple or Pumpkin Cheese Spread

1 T. unsalted butter
½ C. pecans (chopped)
4 (3 oz.) pkgs. cream cheese
   (softened)
1½ C. (6 oz.) sharp Cheddar
   cheese (shredded)
2 garlic cloves (minced)

½ C. (2½ oz.) blue cheese
   (crumbled)
1 C. canned pureed pumpkin
   (fresh) or applesauce
2-4 T. sweet or dry sherry
Crackers for garnish

Line 3½ to 4-cup mold with platic wrap. In small skillet, melt butter. Saute pecans in hot butter 1 minute until golden; set aside. In a large mixer bowl, beat cream cheese, Cheddar cheese, blue cheese, pumpkin and garlic at medium speed of electric mixer until creamy. Beat in enough sherry to make desired spreading consistency. Spoon into mold. Cover and refrigerate 8 hours or overnight until firm enough to hold its shape. To Serve: Unmold spread on serving plate. Peel off plastic wrap. Lightly press pecans atop spread. Surround spread with crackers. Yield: 3½ C.

# Hot Cider Punch

2 C. cranberry juice
8 C. apple cider
¼ C. brown sugar

2 cinnamon sticks
¾ T. whole cloves
¼ tsp. salt

Place juice and cider in electric perculator. Place all other ingredients in basket. Perk till it shuts off. For a 30 cup pot, use 1 gallon cider, 1 quart cranberry juice, and triple spices.

# Apple Juice Punch

3 C. apple cider
4 C. grape juice

1 small bottle ginger ale
Ice

Mix and serve.

# Apple Dips

1 (8 oz.) pkg. cream cheese
1 C. brown sugar

1 tsp. vanilla

Mix together in bowl until smooth. Serve with apple slices or other fruits. (Can soften in microwave on low 1 to 2 minutes.)

OR

1 jar marshmallow creme   OR
1 (8 oz.) pkg. cream cheese
   (softened)
1 tsp. vanilla or 1 T. orange
   juice and grated rind

1 pkg. caramels (unwrapped,
   about 3 lbs.)
¼-½ C. cream or canned milk
2 T. rum or 1 T. water & 1 tsp.
   rum extract

Mix in pan or microwave bowl. Melt caramels using low heat. Good for apple or other fruits, cake or ice cream topping.

# Mulled Cider Punch

2 qt. apple cider or juice
1 C. apricot nectar
1 C. orange juice

½ tsp. cinnamon
Orange slices

In saucepan, combine cider, nectar, orange juice and cinnamon; heat and stir. Garnish with orange slices.

# Hot Apple Cider

2 qt. cider
1 tsp. allspice
1 tsp. whole cloves

1 stick cinnamon
¼ tsp. salt
½ c. brown sugar

Put all ingredients into a large pan and bring to a boil and simmer for 20 minutes. Store leftovers in refrigerator.

# Apple Kabobs

6 medium apples
¼ C. butter
½ tsp. cinnamon

½ tsp. nutmeg
½ tsp. ground ginger
1 T. smooth peanut butter

Core and cut apples in 6 wedges. Cut each wedge in half. Thread on 6 skewers and place in broiling pan. Melt butter and stir in spices and peanut butter. Brush apple chunks with mixture and broil for 4 minutes, basting generously each time the skewers are given a quarter turn. Serve hot.

# Cinnamon Cider

2 qts. apple juice or cider

¼ C. red cinnamon candies

Heat juice and candies together. Serve hot. Makes 8 cups.

# Wassail

1 gal. cider
⅔ C. sugar
2 tsp. whole cloves

2 tsp. whole allspice
2 sticks cinnamon
2 oranges

Heat all ingredients except oranges. Reduce heat, cover and simmer 20 minutes. Strain; pour in serving bowl, float orange slices. Serves 24.

# Apple Cranberry Wassail

1 gal. cranberry juice cocktail
5 C. apple juice
⅔ C. sugar
4 (3-inch) cinnamon sticks

2 tsp. whole allspice
1 medium orange (sliced)
20 whole cloves

Combine cranberry juice cocktail, apple juice, sugar, cinnamon sticks, and allspice in a large pot. Heat to boiling over medium heat; reduce heat and simmer 10 minutes. Strain punch to remove spices. Serve warm in a heat proof punch bowl or chill and serve over ice. Garnish with orange slices studded with cloves. Makes 42 (4 oz.) servings.

# Wassail

1 gal. cider or can apple juice
1 (46 oz.) can unsweetened
  pineapple juice

1 C. orange juice
3 sticks cinnamon
1 tsp. whole cloves

Combine all ingredients in large saucepan. Heat to boiling; reduce heat and simmer 15 to 20 minutes. Remove from heat and strain. Pour hot wassail in heat-proof punch bowl. Garnish with slices of unpeeled apple, studded with cloves, if desired. Makes 24 servings.

# Main Dishes

# Apple Dumplings

Into processor bowl, put:

**2 cubes frozen butter, cut into 4 chunks**    **1 T. sugar**
**2 1/2 c. all-purpose flour**

Process until it is "mealy".

While processing, add ice water a few drops at a time, continuing just until the pastry begins to pull together. Discontinue adding ice water but continue to process until the pastry forms a ball. Remove from processor bowl and divide into four parts, form each into a "patty". Cut one patty into 8 wedges; freeze remaining patties. Form each wedge into a small patty, roll out into a 8- to 9-inch circle on a well-floured board or pastry cloth. Roll them as thin as possible.

**Apples:** Peel and core 8 medium apples. We use Gala or Golden Delicious. Plug the wider end of each apple with softened butter, place butter-side down in the center of pastry circle cradled in your left hand. Fill the center of the apple with sugar/cinnamon mixture, then gently pull the pastry up around the apple with both hands and press to crimp the pastry together. Place in glass pie dish, each dish will hold 5 or 6 apples.

Bake at 350° for 45 to 55 minutes, or until the juices run and the apples soften. Remove apples to individual serving bowls and drizzle juice over the top. Can be served with whipped cream or ice cream.

# Apple Cinnamon Sausage 'n Muffins

1 lb. ground breakfast sausage
1 large apple (cored & cut into
  8 rings)
2 T. water

8 English muffins (split & toasted)
⅓ C. apple jelly
½ C. plain yogurt
1/8 tsp. cinnamon

Shape sausage into 8 patties. Cook on medium heat, turning. Remove from skillet and place apples and water in same skillet. Cover; cook about 3 minutes. Assemble sandwich: Muffin half, apple jelly, yogurt (sprinkle of cinnamon), apple ring, sausage and top with muffin half. Makes 8 servings.

# Sausage-Apple Breakfast

1 1/2 lb. pork sausage patties
1/2 c. dried cherries
6 c. cooking apples, peeled & sliced

1 c. sugar
4 T. butter

CORNBREAD TOPPING:
1 (8 1/2 oz.) pkg. Jiffy cornbread or
  1 1/2 c. cornbread mix

1 egg, beaten
1/2 c. milk
2 T. melted butter

Heat oven to 425°.

Brown sausage patties in skillet. Remove and set aside on paper towels. Discard drippings from skillet. In same skillet, combine apples, cherries, sugar and butter; cook until apples are tender. Tuck sausage under apples. (If you prefer to serve in ovenware pan, such as a quiche pan, spray the pan with Pam, then place sausage in it distributing cooking oil evenly and put apple mixture on top.) You can refrigerate this overnight and then proceed in the morning with the cornbread topping.

In a medium bowl, combine all cornbread topping ingredients; stir until smooth. Pour evenly over sausage mixture. Bake at 425° for 15 to 20 minutes, or until golden brown. Yield: 6 to 8 servings.

# Apple and Sweet Potato

6 med. sweet potatoes
2 med. apples (sliced)
1 lemon

¼ C. oleo
½ tsp. nutmeg
½ C. maple suar

Scrub and cook potatoes in boiling water for about 20 minutes. Cool and peel. Preheat oven to 350°. Slice potatoes into ½-inch ring. Arrange a layer in greased 9x13-inch baking pan. Toss apples with lemon juice, place a single layer on potatoes. Continue layering until all slices have been used. Melt oleo adding nutmeg and syrup. Pour over layers. Bake 30 minutes. Serve hot. Yield: 8-10 servings.

# Polish Sausage Apples

2 T. vegetable oil
2 med. onions (sliced thin)
2 cloves garlic (minced)
1 med. red cabbage (shredded)
4 apples (sliced)
1 T. vinegar

2½ lbs. Polish sausage link
1 bay leaf
1 tsp. thyme
¼ tsp. black pepper
½ C. beef or chicken stock
    (bouillon cubes in water)

In a large pan, saute' onion and garlic in oil 5 minutes; add cabbage and saute' 5 additional minutes. Add sliced apples, sausage and spices, stock and vinegar. Cover pot and bring to a boil. Reduce heat and simmer 30 to 40 minutes. Remove sausage; cut into serving-size portions. Arrange vegetables on serving dish; top with sausage pieces.

# Baked Apples

2 Granny Smith apples
4 tsp. brown sugar
Cinnamon

1/8 c. currants
1/8 c. orange cognac

Core apples and use a grapefruit knife to clean out all the seed coverings. Slice off 1/4-inch of tops and bottoms. Place each in custard cups. Microwave until halfway soft. Drain off excess liquid. Fill cavities with sugar and currants soaked in cognac. Sprinkle cinnamon over tops. Set in warm oven until ready.

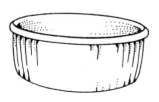

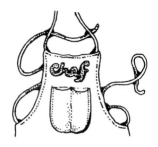

# Piggy Apple

1 c. chopped, peeled apple
2 T. sugar
1 1/2 c. Bisquick
1 1/2 c. milk

4 eggs
2 c. grated Cheddar cheese
6 to 8 slices bacon, cooked & crumbled

Mix apple and sugar; put in greased 7x11-inch pan. Mix Bisquick, milk and eggs just until blended. Pour over apples. Sprinkle with cheese, then bacon. Bake, uncovered, at 375° for 30 to 35 minutes, or until knife comes out clean. Yield: 6 to 8 servings.

# Zapped Apples

1 C. water
⅓ C. brown sugar
1 T. lemon juice
1 tsp. cinnamon
¼ C. apple cider or apple juice
4 large apples

¼ C. brown sugar
¼ C. nuts (chopped)
¼ C. raisins
½ tsp. cinnamon
1 tsp. lemon zest (grated)

In microwave pitcher, combine water with brown sugar, lemon juice and cinnamon on High 3 to 4 minutes. Stir and cook 3 minutes mroe. Stir in apple cider; set aside. Core apples from stem end without cutting through base. Peel apple about ⅓ of the way down from stem end. In small bowl, combine remaining ingredients. Press mixture into center of apples; place apples in round microwave baking dish; pour syrup over apples. Cover loosely with plastic wrap. Microwave on High 12 to 15 minutes or until tender. Baste with syrup halfway through.

# Apple Deep Dish

½ stick butter or margarine
(melted)
¼ C. onion (chopped)
1 C. fresh mushrooms (sliced)
⅓ C. flour
⅔ C. milk

½ tsp. salt
¼ tsp. pepper
1 lb. ham (cut in cubes)
3 C. unpeeled apples (cubed)
1 C. (4 oz.) Cheddar cheese
(shredded)

HERB PASTRY:
Pastry for single crust pie
1 tsp. fresh parsley (chopped)

1 tsp. fresh chives (chopped)

For Herb Pastry: Add fresh parsley and fresh chives to pastry dough. Roll out pastry to extend 1 inch beyond rim of baking dish. Place pastry OVER pie and flute edges at rim of dish.

For Pie: Melt butter; add onion and mushrooms. Cook, stirring until onions are transparent and mushrooms limp. Add milk, flour, salt and pepper; cook until sauce is VERY thick. Sauce will become thin as pie bakes. Combine ham and apple cubes in deep baking dish 1 qt. size. Sprinkle with cheese. Spoon sauce over top. PLACE HERB PASTRY ON TOP. Cut hole in center of pastry to allow steam to escape. Bake at 375° about 45 minutes or until golden brown. Makes 6 to 8 servings.

# Fried Apple Pies

Make a nice rich pastry dough. Cut in 5 or 6 inch squares. Place some cooked apples in and fold over. Moisten edge to make them stick together. Fry in deep fat at about 370° until done. They will be puffed and brown when done. Drain on paper towels to get rid of grease.

# Red Cabbage and Apples

4 c. shredded cabbage
1/2 tsp. salt
1/8 tsp. pepper
2 tsp. sugar
1/2 c. vinegar

1 T. water
1 tsp. butter granules
1 sm. onion, chopped
2 apples, peeled & sliced
3/4 c. hot water

Put cabbage in bowl. Add salt, pepper, sugar and vinegar. Weight down with plate. Refrigerate and allow to stand overnight. Put 1 tablespoon water and butter granules in a large skillet and bring to boil. Sauté onions. Add cabbage and apples. Cook 5 minutes. Add hot water and steam, covered, until tender.
**Yield: 8 servings**

# Maple Apple Rings

4 lg. Granny Smith apples,
    cored & sliced into thin
    rings
3 T. "light" maple syrup

1 T. water
1 tsp. butter granules
1/4 tsp. cinnamon

Prepare apples and set aside. In a large, heavy-bottomed skillet, put maple syrup, water, butter granules and cinnamon. Bring to boil and add apple rings. Cook, uncovered, over medium heat, until tender. Toss very gently, often. Add additional water if needed, however, water should be absorbed when apples are done.
**Yield: 6 servings**

# Baked Apples

Wash and core 1 cooking apple. Place in a sherbet glass, sauce dish, or dish you will serve it in and fill the center with 1 T. brown sugar and 1 tsp. butter; add some red cinnamon candies. Cover with wax paper and microwave for about 2 to 2½ minutes.

# Apple Sausage Patties

1 tsp. olive oil
2 T. finely chopped onion
1 Granny Smith apple
    (peeled, cored & finely)
3 cloves garlic (finely chopped)
½ tsp. dried leaf thyme (crumbled)

½ tsp. ground ginger
1 T. finely chopped fresh sage
    leaves or 1 tsp. dried crumbled
¼ tsp. salt
¼ tsp. black pepper
1 lb. fresh pork sausage
1 egg white

Heat oil in a large nonstick skillet. Add the onion and apple; sauté over medium heat, stirring occasionally, until softened, for about 3 minutes. Stir in the garlic, thyme, ginger, and sage. Remove the skillet from the heat. Stir in the salt and pepper. Let the mixture cool to room temperature. Mix together the apple mixture, sausage, and egg white in a large bowl. Shape the mixture into 12 equal patties. Wipe out the skillet with paper toweling. Working in batches if necessary, add the patties to the skillet. Cook over medium heat until browned and cooked through, about 3 to 4 minutes per side. Serve the patties on biscuits with a little coarse-ground mustard on the side, if desired.

# Pork Chops With Apples

| | |
|---|---|
| 8 pork chops | 5 T. flour |
| 1 tsp. salt | 3 C. hot water |
| 1½ tsp. sage | 3 T. vinegar |
| 4 tart apples (sliced) | ½ C. raisins |
| ½ C. brown sugar | |

Brown chops in skillet; sprinkle with salt and sage. Place in baking dish. Add remaining ingredients, topping with apple slices. Bake at 350° for 1 hour. May need to cover loosely with foil.

# Apple-Glazed Pork Chops

| | |
|---|---|
| 1 can (10¼ ounces) Franco-American beef gravy | 6 pork chops, each cut ¾ inch thick |
| ¼ cup apple jelly | Grapes for garnish |
| 1 tablespoon cider vinegar | Apple slices for garnish |
| ¼ teaspoon ground cloves | Fresh oregano for garnish |
| ⅛ teaspoon pepper | |

1. To make glaze: In 1½-quart saucepan, combine gravy, jelly, vinegar, cloves and pepper. Over medium-high heat, heat to boiling, stirring constantly.

2. On grill rack, place chops directly above medium coals. Grill, uncovered, 20 minutes or until well-done, turning and brushing often with glaze during the last 15 minutes.

3. To serve: Heat any remaining glaze; serve with chops. Garnish with grapes, apple slices and oregano. Makes 6 servings.

***To broil:*** Arrange chops on rack in broiler pan. Broil 4 inches from heat 20 to 30 minutes or until well-done, turning and brushing often with glaze during the last 10 minutes.

# Celery and Apple Stir-Fry

1 tsp. tub margarine, plus
   1 frozen chicken stock
   cube (see index)
3 c. celery, sliced thin
3 c. apples, diced small

1 T. lemon juice
1/4 c. raisins
1/4 tsp. salt (opt.)
1/4 tsp. pepper
1/4 tsp. cinnamon

Sauté apples and celery in margarine and stock. Add lemon juice and cover and cook 3 minutes. Plump raisins in boiling water, then squeeze dry and add to apple mixture. Add salt, pepper and cinnamon and cook until apples and celery are crisp-tender.

**Yield: 6 servings**

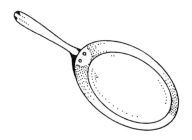

# Fried Apples

4 lg. Granny Smith apples,
   cored & sliced 1/4" thick
1/4 c. water
1 tsp. butter granules

1/4 to 1/2 tsp. cinnamon
Artificial sweetener of choice
   to = 1/3 c. sugar

Put water, butter granules and cinnamon in a skillet and bring to boil. Add apples and cook, over medium heat, uncovered, until tender; tossing often. Liquid should be absorbed when apples are done. Remove from heat and sprinkle with artificial sweetener. Toss to blend.

**Yield: 6 servings**

# Pork 'n Apples

1 C. dry bread crumbs
Fresh parsley (dried or chopped)
1/8 tsp. savory & ½ tsp. sage
  (or poultry seasoning)

1 T. onions (dried)
Salt & pepper (to taste)
6 pork chops
3 tart red apples (diced)

Make dressing, adding water to moisten. Brown chops in skillet. Place in baking pan. Cover with dressing. Bake at 350° for 45 to 60 minutes, covered.

# Apple 'n Pork Chops

1⅔ C. water
⅔ C. apple juice
2 T. butter (divided)
6 oz. long grain wild rice with
  seasoning packet
1 tsp. coriander
½ tsp. salt

¼ tsp. pepper
6 butterflied pork chops
¼ C. apple jelly
1 T. Dijon mustard
1 C. unpeeled red apple (chopped)
⅓ C. toasted almonds

Combine 1 T. butter with first 4 ingredients in saucepan. Bring to boil, reduce heat; cover and simmer about 25 minutes or until liquid is absorbed. Melt 1 T. butter in large skillet, medium heat, 10 minutes, turning once. Remove from skillet. Pour drippings from pan. Combine jelly and mustard in skillet; cook and stir about 2 minutes or until thickened. Pour over cooked chops. Stir apple and almonds into rice.

# **Apple Pie Streusel**

1 unbaked 9-inch pastry shell

MIX TOGETHER IN LARGE BOWL:

½ C. sugar

¼ C. brown sugar

2 T. flour

5 C. peeled sliced fresh apples

2 T. flour

½ tsp. cinnamon

¼ tsp. nutmeg

Toss apples in sugar mixture. Turn apple mixture into pastry shell.

TOP WITH STREUSEL MIX:

¼ C. sugar

¾ C. flour

¼ C. brown sugar

Mix and put in 5 T. butter. Sprinkle on top of apples and bake at 375° for about 55 minutes to 1 hour.

# Apple and Link Sausage

1 lb. link sausage
6 medium onions
Salt
Pepper

Paprika
6 medium sweet potatoes
6 apples
 (pared, cored & halved)

Cover sausage with cold water and boil; drain. Place sausage in large baking dish. Cover with pared sweet potatoes and onions. Season with salt, pepper, and paprika. Cover and bake at 400° for 1 hour; uncover. Add apples and cover. Bake slowly until fruit is tender. Serve at once. Serves 6.

# Apple 'n Red Cabbage

2 T. bacon drippings
4 C. red cabbage (shredded)
2 C. unpeeled apples (cubed)
¼ C. brown sugar
¼ C. vinegar

¼ C. water
1¼ tsp. salt
½ tsp. caraway seed
½ C. golden raisins

Heat drippings in skillet; add remaining ingredients. Cover; cook on low stir occasionally. Cook 15 minutes for crisp cabbage; 25 to 30 minutes fo tender. Makes 4 to 5 servings.

# Apple Ham Casserole

3 C. cooked ham (diced)
2 T. prepared mustard
2 apples (cored & sliced)
2 T. fresh squeezed lemon

½ C. brown sugar
1 tsp. orange rind (grated)
2 T. flour

Arrange ham in 1½ qt. casserole. Spread with mustard. Sprinkle with lemon juice. Arrange cored and sliced apples over ham. Combine brown sugar, orange rind and flour; sprinkle over ham. Bake at 350° for 30 to 35 minutes. Serves 4.

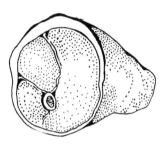

# Apple Three-Bacon Bake

1 tablespoon butter or margarine
1 medium apple, cl.opped
¼ cup finely chopped onion
1 can (16 ounces) Campbell's
   pork & beans in tomato sauce
1 can (10 ounces) kidney beans,
   drained

½ cup cooked butter beans,
   drained
1 tablespoon prepared mustard
Dash pepper
Apple slices for garnish

In 10-inch skillet over medium heat, in hot butter, cook apple and onion until tender, stirring often. Stir in beans, mustard and pepper. Transfer mixture to 1½-quart casserole. Bake, uncovered, at 350°F. 30 minutes or until heated through. Stir before serving. Garnish with apple slices. Makes 4 cups or 6 servings.

*To microwave:* In 1½-quart microwave-safe casserole, combine butter, apple and onion. Microwave, covered, on HIGH 3 minutes or until tender, stirring once. Stir in beans, mustard and pepper. Microwave, covered, on HIGH 7 minutes or until heated through, stirring twice.

# Chicken Salad Sandwiches

2 c. cooked chicken breast,
   chopped
1 med. Granny Smith apple,
   chopped
1/2 c. celery, chopped
1/3 c. green onions, thinly
   sliced
1/4 c. plain nonfat yogurt
1/4 c. light mayonnaise

1/4 c. water chestnuts,
   chopped
2 T. fresh parsley, chopped
2 tsp. lemon juice
1/2 tsp. pepper
1/4 tsp. salt
8 lettuce leaves
8 wholewheat pita pockets

1.   Combine all salad ingredients in a medium bowl and chill.
2.   Line each pocket with a lettuce leaf and fill with 1/2 cup chicken salad.

**Yield: 8 servings**

# Fruit Breakfast

6 T. raisins
6 T. water
1/2 T. almond extract
2 T. apple juice concen-
   trate, undiluted

3 c. low-fat cottage cheese
3 bananas, sliced
3 oranges, sliced
Favorite dry cereal (optional)

1.   Combine raisins, water, almond extract and apple juice concentrate;
   let stand overnight.
2.   In morning, bring mixture to a boil. Reduce heat, cover and let simmer
   10 minutes.
3.   For each serving, place 1/2 cup cottage cheese on serving plate.
4.   Divide sliced fruit evenly among servings. Spoon raisin mixture over
   each.
5.   Top with 3 tablespoons favorite dry cereal if desired.

**Yield: 6 servings**

# Soup

Wow, here we've got a whole section just for soups and have only two soup recipes!

Here we've got this cutesy little illustration showing this old fashioned gal with a cart and a couple of dogs, and we have only two recipes.

What we need is a couple more recipes to put on page 40.

If any of you readers out there have any really good soup recipes using apples, let us know and we'll stick 'em on page 40 next printing along with some words saying all kinds of nice things about you.

That's cheaper, of course than actually flat out paying for them.

They've got to be good recipes to go along with the other knock-your-socks-off apple recipes in this book.

# Apple Soup

1/4 c. water
1 tsp. butter granules
1 med. onion, diced
3 med. apples, peeled, cored
   & sliced
1 carrot, sliced thin
1 green pepper, seeded &
   diced

1 rib celery, diced
2 whole cloves
1 tsp. curry powder
Pinch of ground nutmeg
6 c. chicken stock
1/4 tsp. pepper

Put water and butter granules in a 6-quart saucepan and bring to boil. Add onion and sauté until soft (about 10 minutes). Add apples, carrots, green pepper and celery. Sauté until soft. Add more water, if needed. Add cloves, curry and nutmeg. Stir in chicken stock and add salt and pepper. Cover and simmer 30 to 40 minutes. Remove from stove and purée in blender, in batches. Pour into bowl. Cover and allow to cool. Refrigerate at least 6 hours. Serve in stemmed glasses or cups.
Yield: 8 servings

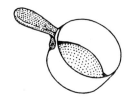

# Apple Cheese Soup

1 C. apple (grated)
¼ C. onion (chopped)
4 T. butter
¼ C. flour
2½ C. milk

⅔ C. apple cider
2 C. sharp Cheddar cheese
   (shredded)
¼ tsp. salt
½ tsp. nutmeg

Cook apples and onions in butter until tender. Add flour and salt and blend until smooth. Add milk and cider and cook until thickened. Add cheese over medium heat until melted. Serve.

# Salads

# Cinnamon Applesauce Jell-O

1 (3 oz.) pkg. red Jell-o
1 C. boiling water
¼ C. cold water

1 C. applesauce
½ tsp. cinnamon
1 C. Cool Whip

Combine Jell-o with boiling water and stir until dissolved. Add cold water. Pour 1 C. of jell-o mixture into applesauce/cinnamon mixture; chill. Stir in remaining Jell-o and add to 1 C. Cool Whip. Use this last to frost gelatin salad.

# Apple Salad

8 C. tart red
    apples (chopped, unpeeled)
1 (20 oz.) can pineapple chunks
    (drain & reserve juice)

1 C. seedless red grapes
1 C. seedless green grapes
1 to 2 tsp. poppy seed
1½ C. toasted pecans

DRESSING:
Reserved pineapple juice
¼ C. sugar
2 T. cornstarch
½ C. lite mayonnaise

¼ C. butter
1 T. lemon juice
2 T. water
½ C. plain yogurt

Combine the pineapple juice, butter, sugar, and lemon juice in a 2-quart saucepan. Add the cornstarch that has been dissolved in the water to the juice mixture. Cook over a medium heat until thick, stirring constantly; cool. Mix the apples, pineapple, grapes, poppy seed, and nuts. Fold the cooled pineapple juice mixture in with the mayonnaise and the yogurt. Toss the dressing with the fruit mixture. Serve in lettuce leaves or in fruit cups. Makes 12 servings.

# Orange, Apple and Cabbage Slaw

4 C. shredded savoy cabbage
2 large eating apples
1 T. sugar
½ C. orange juice

2 T. lemon juice
¾ C. heavy cream
Salt & pepper
Mandarin oranges

Prepare cabbage according to standard directions for cole slaw. Quarter and core but do not peel apples. Cut in thin slices and add to cabbage. Mix well with sugar and fruit juices. Whip cream until stiff and fold into salad; add salt and pepper, to taste. Cover and chill in refrigerator. Toss again before serving and garnish with mandarin oranges.

# Apple Salad

½ C. mayonnaise
¼ C. honey
¼ C. peanut butter
1 apple (cored & diced)

1 carrot (grated)
¼ C. celery (thinly sliced)
¼ C. raisins
¼ C. chopped peanuts

Combine mayonnaise, honey, and peanut butter. Stir in remaining ingredients and chill.

# Apple 'n Chicken Salad

1 medium apple (cored & chopped)
1 C. diced cooked chicken
2 to 4 T. regular or light mayonnaise
2 T. diced green pepper
1 tsp. chopped pimiento

Dash dried rosemary (crushed)
Dash lemon pepper
Lettuce leaf
Alfalfa sprouts (optional)

In a small bowl, combine first seven ingredients. Chill until ready to serve. Place lettuce leaf on a serving plate and top with the chilled chicken salad.

# Poppy Seed Apple Salad

DRESSING:
¼ C. sugar
2 T. cornstarch
1 C. reserved pineapple juice
  (see below)
1 T. lemon juice

¼ C. butter or margarine (cut into
  pieces)
½ C. plain yogurt
½ C. mayonnaise

SALAD:
8 C. Red Delicious apples
  (unpared, chopped)
1 (20 oz.) can pineapple chunks
  (drained, reserve juice)

1½ C. toasted pecan halves
1-2 tsp. poppy seeds
1 C. seedless green grapes
1 C. seedless red grapes

For Dressing: In 1 qt. saucepan, combine sugar and cornstarch. If necessary add water to reserved pineapple juice to make 1 C. Gradually blend pineapple juice into sugar mixture. Cook over medium heat, stirring constantly, until mixture is thickened and bubbling. Remove from heat. Stir in butter or margarine and lemon juice until smooth. Lay a piece of plastic wrap directly on top of dressing to prevent a ''skin'' from forming; chill. Fold yogurt and mayonnaise into cooled dressing.

For Salad: In extra large bowl, combine all salad ingredients. Pour dressing over salad, tossing to coat. Serve on lettuce-lined plates or in fruit cups. Makes 12 servings.

# Chicken Salad Supreme

**DRESSING:**
1/2 c. plain nonfat yogurt

1/4 c. light mayonnaise
1/4 tsp. cinnamon

**SALAD:**
16 oz. chicken breast strips
3/4 c. apple juice
3/4 c. water
1/2 c. long grain & wild rice, uncooked
3/4 c. McIntosh apple, unpeeled & chopped

1/2 c. celery, sliced
1/2 c. water chestnuts, chopped
30 seedless green grapes, cut into halves
Spinach leaves to garnish (optional)

1. Cook rice according to package directions.
2. Wash chicken pieces; pat dry. Set aside.
3. To prepare dressing, combine all ingredients in a small bowl; cover and refrigerate.
4. In a 2-quart saucepan, simmer chicken, apple juice and water, covered, over medium heat 15 to 20 minutes until juice runs clear when meat is pierced with fork. Remove chicken from pan and reserve juices for cooking rice.
5. Cut chicken in half-inch cubes; cover and chill.
6. Cook long grain and wild rice in cooking juices from chicken, adding water as needed, following label directions.
7. In a large bowl, gently toss together rice, apple, celery, water chestnuts and grapes; stir in chicken and dressing.
8. Serve on spinach leaves.

**Yield: 6 servings**

# Fruit Salad

2 apples (red)
1 bananas
1 green apple
2 pears
½ lb. red grapes
½ C. slivered almonds (toasted)

1 C. vanilla yogurt
1 tsp. cinnamon
¼ tsp. ginger
¼ tsp. nutmeg
1 T. apple cider, apple juice or apple vinegar

Wash and core apples and pears, cut in 1-inch chunks. Slice bananas. Wash grapes and cut in half. Combine fruits and almonds in salad bowl. Mix yogurt with spices and cider. Pour over fruit, mix and chill. Serves 8.

# Apple Waldorf Salad

1 Granny Smith apple
1 red delicious apple
1 T. lemon juice
1/2 c. celery, chopped
1 T. pecan halves, slightly
    chopped

1/4 c. plain nonfat yogurt
Dash of cinnamon
Dash of nutmeg
1 T. light mayonnaise
Purple cabbage or lettuce
    leaves (optional)

1. Chop unpeeled apples; sprinkle with lemon juice.
2. Add all other ingredients; combine gently.
3. Serve on purple cabbage leaf or lettuce leaf.

**Yield: 4 servings**

# Tuna Salad

1 (6 1/2 oz.) can water-
    packed tuna, drained
2 T. light mayonnaise
1 T. lemon juice

1 celery stalk, diced
1 green onion, diced
2 T. apple, diced
3 sm. or 1 lg. sweet pickle

1. Combine all ingredients.

**Yield: 3 servings**
**Per Serving** (1/2 cup):
    152 cal, 4 gm fat, 17 gm pro, 13 gm carb, 11 mg chol, 397 mg sodium,
    1 gm dietary fiber

# Lazy Lady Apple Salad

3 med. apples, cored & diced
1 banana, peeled & sliced
1 c. seedless grapes, halved

1 (16 oz.) can crushed
    pineapple, drained
6 oz. "light" Cool Whip
2 T. "free" no-fat mayonnaise

Put all of fruit in a mixing bowl. Combine Cool Whip and mayonnaise. Pour into fruit and gently toss.
**Yield: 8 servings**

*Approximate Per Serving:*
Calories: 82
Fat: 2.0 g
Cholesterol: 0.0 mg

Carbohydrates: 18.9 g
Protein: 0.2 g
Sodium: 49 mg

Exchanges: 2 fruit

# Easy Apple Salad

4 tender-skinned delicious
    apples, washed & diced
1/2 c. raisins, plumped (put
    in boiling water for 10
    minutes, squeeze dry)

1 (16 oz.) can fruit cocktail,
    water packed; drain &
    reserve juice
1/2 c. "yogurt cheese" (see
    index), can use plain
    low-fat yogurt
1 T. honey

Combine apples, raisins and drained fruit cocktail. Mix yogurt and honey and pour over fruit. Gently stir to blend. Chill 1 hour before serving.
**Yield: 8 servings**

# Apple Swirl Salad

1/4 c. cinnamon candies
2 c. boiling water
2 (3 oz.) pkg. raspberry
   gelatin, reg. or sugar-free
2 c. unsweetened applesauce

1 c. dry cottage cheese
1 T. tub margarine
1 tsp. lemon juice
2 T. reduced-calorie
   mayonnaise

Dissolve candies in boiling water. Add gelatin and stir until dissolved. Add applesauce and chill until mixture begins to thicken. Combine cottage cheese, margarine, lemon juice and mayonnaise and process in blender until smooth. Spoon cheese mixture on top of gelatin mixture that has begun to thicken. Swirl with a spoon for a marbled effect. Pour into a ring mold or an 8x8-inch dish. Return to refrigerator until set. Cut in 2x4-inch squares.
**Yield: 8 servings**

# Applesauce Salad

1/2 c. boiling water
1 (3 oz.) pkg. lemon Jello

1/4 c. red hot candies
1 (16 oz.) can applesauce

Add gelatin and red hots to boiling water and heat until candies are dissolved. Stir in applesauce and pour into a 3-cup mold that has been lightly sprayed with vegetable oil. Chill until set.
**Yield: 8 servings**

# Apple 'n Raisin Slaw

1½ C. unpeeled, cored & diced
   red apples
2 C. shredded cabbage

⅓ C. seedless raisins
½ C. coleslaw dressing

Mix thoroughly the apples, cabbage, raisins, and dressing. Serves 4.

# Cinnamon Apple Rings

3 C. hot tap water
1½ C. sugar
½ C. red cinnamon candies
¼ tsp. salt
4 med. apples

1 (3 oz., pkg. cream cheese
¼ C. nuts or green pepper
 (chopped)
Lettuce leaves

In 2-qt. glass measuring pitcher or casserole, combine water, sugar, cinnamon candies and salt. Microwave, covered, on High (100%) for 10 to 14 minutes or until boiling. Add apples. Microwave, covered, on Medium (50%) for 7 to 10 minutes or until apples are tender. Do not overcook. turn apples over halfway through cooking time to color evenly. Chill apples in the syrup; drain. In small glass bowl, place cream cheese. Microwave on low (30%) for 45 seconds to 1½ minutes or until softened. Stir in nuts or green pepper. Stuff the apples with cream cheese mixture. Chill until serving time. to serve, cut each apple in half crosswise. Arrange on lettuce lined plates. Makes 4 servings.

# Apple Rings

3-4 lg. apples

Syrup:

2 c. sugar
1 c. water
½ c. vinegar

1 stick cinnamon
6 whole cloves
Red food coloring

Core apples and slice in rings about ½ inch thick, do not peel apples. Prepare boiling syrup in a pan, mix sugar, water, vinegar, cinnamon stick and whole cloves and red food coloring. Boil apples slowly in this syrup turning until they are done. Cool in syrup.

# Applesauce Jell-O Salad

½ C. red cinnamon candies
1 (3 oz.) pkg. lemon flavor
gelatin
1 C. boiling water
1½ C. sweetened applesauce

1 (8 oz.) pkg. cream cheese
(softened)
½ C. nuts (choppped)
½ C. celery (chopped)
½ C. mayonnaise

Dissolve cinnamon candies and gelatin in boiling water. Add applesauce; mix well. Pour half of mixture in 8-inch square baking pan. Chill until firm. Let remaining gelatin mixture stand at room temperature. Stir cream cheese until smooth. Add nuts and celery; mix well. Stir in mayonnaise. Spread over chilled gelatin layer. Pour remaining gelatin mixture evenly on top. Chill until firm. Cut in squares. Makes 6 servings.

# Applesauce Salad

2 1/2 c. boiling water
2 (3 oz.) pkg. lemon gelatin
1 (16 oz.) can unsweetened
applesauce
1 tsp. cinnamon

1 (8 oz.) pkg. "free" no-fat
Philadelphia cream cheese
2 T. skim milk
1/2 tsp. lemon extract

Dissolve gelatin in boiling water. Add applesauce and cinnamon. Pour into 8x8-inch baking dish and chill until set. Blend cream cheese, milk and lemon extract. Spread over gelatin.
**Yield: 9 servings**

# Waldorf Salad

¼ C. plain yogurt
¼ C. mayonnaise
1 tsp. lemon juice
½ tsp. sugar
¼ tsp. ground ginger
Lettuce leaves

1 large Red Delicious apple
1 large Golden Delicious apple
¼ C. celery (sliced)
¼ C. pecans or walnuts (coarsely chopped)

In small bowl, combine yogurt, mayonnaise, lemon juice, sugar and ginger. Stir the mixture until smooth. Set aside. Arrange lettuce leaves on 4 salad plates. Core apples and cut into ½-inch thick slices. Arrange apple slices on lettuce. Sprinkle with celery and nuts. Serve with dressing on the side. Makes 4 servings.

# Apple In A Pocket

1 apple (chopped)
1 celery rib (sliced)
1 tsp. lemon juice
1 small onion (chopped)
1 (7 oz.) can tuna (drained)

1 tsp. dill weed (dried)
½ C. mayonnaise
4 small pita bread pockets
4 large lettuce leaves

Mix salad ingredients. Place lettuce leaf in each pita pocket; stuff with tuna mixture and serve.

# Apple-Tuna Salad

1 (6½-7 oz.) can tuna fish
  (packed in water)
1 unpeeled apple (diced)
1 stalk celery (chopped)

2 T. mayonnaise
1 T. lemon juice
Lettuce as desired

Rinse and drain tuna. Mix tuna and other ingredients, except lettuce in bowl. Use immediately or chill 1 to 2 hours. Serve on bed of lettuce leaves. Makes 4 servings, about ½ C. each with 126 calories per serving. VARIATIONS: Oil-packed instead of water-packed tuna may be used. Pour oil from tuna can, rinse tuna with cold water, and drain well.

# Apple Carrot Salad

2 C. carrots (shredded)
1 C. unpeeled apples (diced)
½ C. raisins

1 tsp. lemon juice
Salad dressing

Combine carrots, apples, raisins and lemon juice. Add enough salad dressing to moisten. Chill. Makes 4 to 5 servings.

# Breads

# Apple Muffins

1¾ C. flour
½ C. sugar
⅓ C. brown sugar
¾ C. milk
¼ C. shortening
½ C. nutmeats (chopped)

2 tsp. baking powder
1 egg (well beaten)
1¼ C. apple (chopped)
1 tsp. cinnamon
½ tsp. salt

Combine flour, sugar, baking powder, salt, ½ tsp. cinnamon and milk; mix well. Mix in eggs shortening and apples. Put batter into greased muffin pan or cups. Stir together brown sugar, nutmeats and ½ tsp. cinnamon to sprinkle on top. Bake in 360° oven for about 20-25 minutes.

# Apple Fritters

1 C. flour
1½ tsp. baking powder
½ tsp. salt
1 egg (beaten)

½ to ¾ C. milk
1 T. melted margarine
1 T. sugar
1 C. peeled and diced tart apples

Sift dry ingredients together. Combine rest of ingredients and add to the dry mixture. Use right amount of milk to make right consistency batter. Fry in deep hot fat (365-375°) til done, which will take about 5 minutes. Sprinkle with powdered sugar.

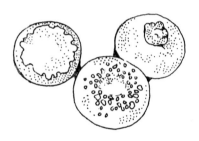

# Apple Rolls

½ C. sugar
1¼ tsp. salt
¼ C. shortening
3¼ C. flour (sifted)
1 well beaten egg
2 C. apples (sliced)
Milk

2 pkgs. yeast (dissolved in ⅔ C. hot water
1 C. brown sugar
2 tsp. cinnamon
¼ C. melted butter
¾ C. powdered sugar

Blend together sugar, salt, shortening and egg; stir in yeast/water. Mix in flour; beat for 2 minutes. Set aside and let rise until double. Roll dough out in a rectangle, brush with melted butter and sprinkle with a mixture of brown sugar and cinnamon. Lay apple slices over dough; roll up tightly. Slice roll and lay pieces on greased pan, then let set to rise for 1 hour. Bake for 25 minutes at 400°. Glaze with a mixture of powdered sugar and enough milk to make just the right consistency.

# Applesauce Bread

1 c. applesauce, unsweet-
   ened
1 c. sugar
1/4 c. vegetable oil
4 egg whites
3 T. skim milk
1/2 c. raisins
1 c. flour

1 c. wholewheat flour
1 tsp. baking soda
1/2 tsp. baking powder
3/4 tsp. cinnamon
1/4 tsp. salt
1/2 tsp. nutmeg
Nonstick vegetable
   cooking spray

TOPPING (Optional):
2 T. pecans, chopped

1/2 c. brown sugar
1/2 tsp. cinnamon

1. Preheat oven to 350°F.
2. Combine applesauce, sugar, oil, egg whites, milk and raisins.
3. Sift together flours, baking soda, baking powder, cinnamon, salt and nutmeg.
4. Stir flour into applesauce mixture and mix well.
5. Pour into loaf pan sprayed with cooking spray.
6. Combine pecans, brown sugar and cinnamon; sprinkle over batter.
7. Bake for 1 hour.

**Yield: 16 servings**

# Carrot Oatmeal Muffins

1 c. buttermilk, skim
1 c. dry oatmeal
1/4 c. brown sugar
2 egg whites or 1/4 c. egg
   substitute
1 c. carrots, finely grated
1/2 c. raisins

1 tsp. cinnamon
1/2 c. applesauce
1/4 c. nonfat plain yogurt
   (optional)
1/2 c. oat bran, dry
1 c. wholewheat flour
1 tsp. baking soda

1. Mix buttermilk and oatmeal and let stand until liquid is absorbed.
2. Add sugar, egg whites, carrots, raisins, cinnamon, applesauce and yogurt (if desired). Mix well.
3. Stir together remaining dry ingredients and mix with wet ingredients.
4. Spray muffin tins with cooking spray and fill 2/3 full.
5. Bake at 375°F. for about 22 minutes.

# French Toast With

# Fried Apple Topping

**FRIED APPLES:**
4 T. butter, melted
2 T. sugar

6 c. apples, peeled & sliced
2 T. brown sugar
Pinch of salt

**CARAMEL FRENCH TOAST:**
1 c. packed brown sugar
1/3 c. butter
2 T. light corn syrup

6 (1" thick) slices French bread
5 eggs
1 1/2 c. milk
1 tsp. cinnamon

Powdered sugar, for dusting

**French Toast:** In a small saucepan, combine the brown sugar, butter and corn syrup. Cook over medium heat, stirring constantly, until butter melts. Pour the brown sugar mixture into an ungreased 9x13-inch glass baking dish. Arrange the bread slices over the top of the brown sugar mixture. Set aside.

Beat the eggs, milk and cinnamon in a bowl until combined. Pour the liquid over the bread, saturating all the slices. Cover and refrigerate at least 2 hours or overnight. Preheat oven to 350°. Uncover the bread and bake for 30 to 35 minutes, or until the center appears set and the top is lightly browned. Let stand about 10 minutes before serving. Top with fried apples and powdered sugar. Yield: 6 servings.

# Apple Dumplin's

Make a rich biscuit dough, the same as soda or baking powder biscuit, only adding a little more shortening. Take a piece of dough out on the molding-board, roll out almost as thin as pie crust; then cut into square pieces large enough to cover an apple. Put into the middle of each piece two apple halves that have been pared and cored; sprinkle on a spoonful of sugar and a pinch of ground cinnamon, turn the ends of the dough over the apple and lap them tight.

Lay dumplings in a dripping pan (buttered), the smooth side upward. When the pans are filled, put a small piece of butter on top of each, sprinkle over a large handful of sugar,pour in a cup of boiling water, then place in a moderate oven for three-quarters of an hour. Baste with brandy once while baking. Serve with pudding, sauce or cream and sugar.

# Apple Bread

½ C. oil
2 eggs
1 C. sugar
1½ C. all-purpose flour
½ tsp. baking soda
1½ C. diced peeled apples

¼ tsp. salt
½ C. chopped nuts
1 tsp. vanilla
½ tsp. cinnamon
½ tsp. nutmeg

Mix first 3 ingredients together. Add remaining ingredients and mix. Turn into greased and floured 8x4-inch loaf pan. Bake at 300° for 1½ hours. Cool for 10 minutes. Remove from pan. Cool on rack for 10 minutes. Wrap in foil while still warm.

# Apple Nut Bread

1½ C. oil
2 C. sugar
4 eggs
3 C. flour
1 tsp. cinnamon

½ tsp. salt (optional)
1 tsp. baking soda
1 tsp. vanilla
3 C. chopped peeled apples
1 C. chopped nuts (optional)

Beat together oil and sugar; add eggs, dry ingredients and remaining ingredients. Bake in 2 greased loaf pans at 325° for 1 hour.

# Apple Raisin Loaves

3 eggs
2 C. chopped raw apples
1 tsp. vanilla
2 tsp. baking soda
1 tsp. salt
1 tsp. cloves

1½ C. oil
1½ C. sugar
3⅓ C. flour
1 tsp. baking powder
1 tsp. cinnamon
⅔ C. raisins

Heat oven to 350°. Grease and flour 2 loaf pans. Beat eggs, oil, apples, sugar and vanilla on low speed, 1 minute. Add flour, soda, baking powder, salt, cinnamon and cloves. Beat on low speed about 15 seconds. Beat on medium speed 45 seconds. Stir in nuts and raisins. Spread in pans. Bake 55 to 60 minutes or until done. Cool completely before slicing.

# Pumpkin Apple Pancakes

1 lg. red Delicious apple,
   peeled, cored & sliced thin
1 T. water
1/2 tsp. butter granules
1/2 c. yellow cornmeal
1 c. boiling water
1 c. skim milk
1/2 c. canned pumpkin

Egg substitute to = 2 eggs
1 c. flour, whole wheat blend,
   unbleached or enriched
   all-purpose flour
1 T. sugar
2 1/2 tsp. baking powder
1 tsp. allspice
1/2 tsp. salt (less if desired)

In skillet, over medium heat, put water and butter granules. Stir until butter granules dissolve. Add apples and sauté until softened (3 or 4 minutes). Remove from heat and keep warm. In a large mixing bowl, mix cornmeal and boiling water. Allow to stand 5 minutes. Add milk, pumpkin and egg substitute; blend well. Blend together flour, sugar, baking powder, allspice and salt. Add to pumpkin mixture and stir just until moistened. Cook pancakes on griddle or in heavy bottomed skillet sprayed with cooking oil. When bubbles form on top, turn and cook second side. Keep warm. Put in stacks of flour and top with apples.

**Yield: 6 servings**

# Apple Oatmeal Muffins

1 egg
¾ C. milk
1 C. raisins
1 C. chopped apples
½ C. oil
1 C. all-purpose flour

1 C. oatmeal
⅓ C. sugar
3 tsp. baking powder
1 tsp. salt
1 tsp. nutmeg
2 tsp. cinnamon

Beat egg and stir in remaining ingredients, mixing just to moisten. Pour int 12 greased muffin cups until ¾ full. Bake at 400° for 15 to 20 minutes. Serv cool or hot with butter.

# Apple Syrup

*Wonderful on French toast, waffles, pancakes, ginger bread.*

16 oz. thawed apple juice concentrate
16 oz. water
2 1/2 c. sugar

2 tsp. cinnamon
1/4 tsp. ground cloves

Thicken with rue (3 tablespoons cornstarch mixed with 1/4 cup water). Put apple juice concentrate and water in 4-quart pan on medium. In a separate container, stir sugar, cinnamon and cloves together. Add to apple juice on stove and bring to a low boil for 1 minute. Stir in cornstarch mix and boil for 1 additional minute.

Microwaves nicely. Best when served warm.

This will store very well in the refrigerator for 2 or 3 months – it will separate but is easily stirred back together.

# Coffee Cake

1 C. granulated sugar
1 C. oil
4 eggs

2 C. all-purpose flour
1 tsp. baking powder
1 can cherry pie filling

Cream sugar and oil. Add unbeaten eggs. Sift dry ingredients and add to creamed mixture. Put ½ mixture into 9x13-inch pan and pour pie mix over. Spread remaining batter over pie mix and sprinkle with cinnamon and sugar. Bake at 350° for 30 minutes. Drizzle with powdered sugar frosting when cool.

# Applesauce-Carrot Muffins

½ C. raisins
1 C. all-purpose flour
¾ C. whole-wheat flour
1 tsp. baking soda
½ tsp. salt
1 tsp. cinnamon
½ tsp. nutmeg (optional)

1 large egg
½ C. sugar
¼ C. oil
1 tsp. vanilla
¼ tsp. lemon extract
1 C. applesauce
¾ C. grated carrots.

Combine raisins with ½ C. warm water in small bowl; let soak. Mix flours, soda, salt, and spices in large bowl. Beat egg and sugar in second bowl until fluffy; beat in oil, vanilla, and lemon. Stir in applesauce. Stir applesauce mixture into flour until just blended. Quickly fold in carrots and raisins with water; spoon into greased or sprayed muffin tins. Bake at 400° for 15 to 18 minutes. Makes 12 large muffins.

# Applesauce Filled Pancakes

Egg substitute to = 2 eggs
1/4 tsp. salt (less if desired)
1 1/4 c. flour, whole wheat
    blend, unbleached or
    enriched all-purpose flour

2 c. skim milk
1/4 tsp. vanilla extract
1/4 tsp. almond extract
2 c. pink unsweetened
    applesauce

In a mixing bowl, put egg substitute and salt. Add flour, 1/2 cup milk and extracts. Beat until smooth. While beating, add remaining milk. Spray a 6-inch skillet with cooking spray and add 2 table-spoons batter to skillet, and tilt skillet so entire skillet surface is coated (as you would for a crepe). Cook until bubbles form; turn for 1 minute. Keep warm while remaining are cooked. Stack pancakes, spreading each pancake with applesauce. Pour remaining applesauce over top of stack. Cut into 4 wedges.
**Yield: 4 servings**

# Apple Raisin Pancakes

1 1/2 c. flour, whole wheat blend, unbleached or enriched all-purpose
6 pkt. Equal or artificial sweetener of choice to = 1/4 c. sugar
2 tsp. baking powder
1/4 tsp. salt (less if desired)
1/2 tsp. ground allspice
1/2 tsp. cinnamon
1 1/4 c. skim milk (room temp.)
Egg substitute to = 2 eggs
1/4 tsp. vanilla
1/4 c. hot water
1 tsp. butter granules
4 lg. Granny Smith apples, peeled, cored & sliced
1/2 c. raisins
3/4 tsp. cinnamon
5 pkt. sweetener, or sweetener of choice to = 3 T. sugar

In a mixing bowl, sift flour, sweetener, baking powder, salt, allspice and cinnamon. In a second bowl, put 1 cup milk, egg substitute and vanilla. Stir wet ingredients into dry ingredients just until moistened. Cover and chill 5 hours.

In a heavy-bottomed skillet, put water and butter granules and bring to boil. Add apples, raisins and 3/4 teaspoon cinnamon and cook until soft, stirring several times. Remove from heat and add sweetener. Set aside, keeping warm.

Stir chilled batter and thin with remaining milk. Using 1/2 cup batter for each pancake, cook on hot griddle or in heavy-bottomed skillet over moderate heat until bubbles cover top. Turn and cook second side. Put pancakes on hot serving plate and top with hot apples.
Yield: 6 pancakes

# Fresh Apple Fritters

1 c. flour
1/4 tsp. salt
2 T. sugar
1 1/2 tsp. baking powder
1 egg
1/2 c. milk
3 apples, sliced or chopped

Sift together the flour, salt, sugar and baking powder. Stir in egg (beaten), milk and apples. Drop by tablespoon into hot grease or oil (375°) and fry slowly until brown. Drain on paper towels and then roll in sugar or powdered sugar. Best eaten when warm.

# No Oil Cherry Muffins

3 egg whites, beaten
1 cup sugar
1 1/2 cups flour
1 1/2 tsp. baking powder
1/2 tsp. salt
1 cup chopped nuts
1 jar (8 oz.) maraschino cherries,
    drained, but save juice

In large bowl beat egg whites; add sugar and beat again. Add cherry juice and stir. Stir in nuts, cherries, flour, salt, and baking powder. Fold in egg whites. Spoon batter into prepared muffin tins. Bake at 350 degrees for about 25 minutes.

# Apple Muffins

1 1/2 c. unbleached flour or
    enriched all-purpose flour
1/2 c. sugar
2 tsp. baking powder
1/2 tsp. salt (opt.)
1/2 tsp. nutmeg
1/4 c. tub margarine
Egg substitute to equal
    1 egg or 2 egg whites
1/2 c. skim milk
1/2 c. apples, peeled,
    cored & finely chopped

Mix dry ingredients and cut in margarine until the consistency of cornmeal. Combine egg substitute, milk and apples. Stir into dry ingredients, mixing until well blended. Spoon into 12 muffin tins that have been lined with foil muffin liners; or spray muffin pans with vegetable oil. Fill two-thirds full. Bake at 350° in a preheated oven for 20 to 25 minutes. If desired, brush top with orange juice and dip into a mixture of cinnamon and sugar. **Yield: 12 muffins. Serving size: 1 muffin**

# Dutch Apple Bread

½ C. shortening (no butter)
1 C. granulated sugar
2 eggs
1 C. coarsely chopped apples
    (peeled)
2 C. all-purpose flour (sifted)
1½ T. sour milk
1 tsp. baking soda
½ tsp. salt
1 tsp. vanilla

Cream shortening and sugar; add the eggs and beat. Add the chopped apples. Add the flour and beat well. Mix the sour milk with the soda. Add to batter. Add the salt and vanilla; beat. Put in two 4x8-inch greased pans. Top with mixture of 2 tablespoons and ½ tsp. cinnamon. Bake at 350° for 50 to 60 minutes. NOTE: Nutmeats may also be added.

# Sourdough Apple Muffins

1 1/2 c. whole wheat blend or enriched all-purpose flour
1/4 c. sugar
2 tsp. baking powder
1/2 tsp. salt
1 tsp. cinnamon
Egg substitute to = 1 egg
1/2 c. sourdough starter
2/3 c. skim milk
1/3 c. unsweetened applesauce
1 c. peeled, cored & finely-chopped apples

In a mixing bowl, blend flour, sugar, baking powder, salt and cinnamon. With the back of a spoon, make a well in flour mixture. In a second bowl, blend egg substitute, sourdough starter, milk, applesauce and chopped apples. Pour into well in flour mixture. Stir with wooden spoon just until moistened. Spray 12 muffin tins with cooking spray and fill 2/3-full. Bake in 400° preheated oven 20 to 25 minutes, or until done.
**Yield: 12 muffins**

# Fat-Free Carrot Muffins

4 egg whites, beaten
2 cups flour
1 1/2 cups sugar
2 tsp. baking soda
1 tbsp. baking powder
2 tsp. cinnamon
1/2 tsp. salt
1 cup applesauce
2 tsp. vanilla extract
2 cups raw carrots, grated

In a medium size bowl beat egg whites; set aside. In a large bowl combine flour, sugar, baking soda, baking powder, cinnamon, and salt. In a separate bowl mix together applesauce, vanilla, and carrots. Pour wet ingredients into dry mixture; stir just until moist. Fold in egg whites and let stand for 20 minutes. Spray muffin tins with a nonfat cooking spray. Fill greased muffin cups 2/3 full. Bake at 350 degrees for approximately 30 minutes or until golden brown.

# Apple Breakfast Loaf

1¾ C. water
1 C. whole-bran cereal
¼ C. butter or margarine
5½-6 C. all-purpose flour
⅓ C. light brown sugar (firmly packed)

2 pkgs. rapid rise yeast (yeast that requires only 1 rising)
1½ tsp. salt
¾ tsp. ground nutmeg
2 C. (about 2 apples) apples (finely chopped)

ICING:
1 C. confectioners sugar

1-2 T. apple juice concentrate or lemon juice

Heat water, bran and butter until very warm, 125°-130°; let stand 5 minutes. Meanwhile, in a large bowl, combine 1 C. of the flour, the sugar, undissolved yeast, salt and nutmeg. Stir bran mixture into dry ingredients. Stir in apple and enough remaining flour to make soft dough. Knead on lightly floured surface until smooth and elastic, about 6 to 8 minutes. Cover, let rest 10 minutes. Divide dough in ½. On lightly floured surface, roll each ½ to a 12x17-inch rectangle. Roll each up tightly from short end as for a jelly roll. Pinch seams and ends to seal. Place each loaf, seam side down in greased 8½x4½x2½-inch loaf pan. Cover, let rise in warm, draft-free place until doubled in size, about 30 to 45 minutes. Bake in a 375° oven for 40 minutes or until done. Remove from pans; cool on wire rack. Drizzle with icing.

# Apple Bread With Sour Cream

½ C. oleo
1 C. sugar
2 eggs
2 T. sour cream
1 tsp. soda

2 C. flour
½ tsp. salt
2 C. apples (chopped fine)
½ C. nuts/raisins

Mix in order of ingredients; top with 2 T. sugar, 1 tsp. cinnamon, 2 T. flour and 2 T. oleo crumbled over batter. Bake at 350° for 1 hour.

# Applesauce Nut Bread

2 C. flour
¾ C. sugar
1 tsp. baking powder
1 tsp. salt
½ tsp. baking soda

½ tsp. nutmeg
½ tsp. cinnamon
1 C. pecans (chopped)
1 egg (beaten)
1 C. applesauce

Combine all ingredients in a large bowl. Stir just enough to moisten. Pour batter into a greased loaf pan. Bake in a preheated, 300° oven 1 hour or until done.

# Apple Honey Muffins

2 C. flour (sifted)
2 tsp. baking powder
½ tsp. salt
½ C. butter
1 egg (beaten)
Milk
2 T. butter (melted)

¼ C. thick applesauce
2 T. brown sugar (firmly packed)
¼ C. sunflower seeds
¼ C. raisins
⅓ C. brown sugar (firmly packed
¼ C. honey
2 T. butter

Sift flour, baking powder and salt together. Cut in ½ C. butter. Add enough milk to egg to make ⅔ C. Slowly add to flour mixture to form a soft dough. Knead dough ½ minute and roll to 14x10-inch rectangle. Mix together 2 T. butter, applesauce, 2 T. brown suar, sunflower seeds and raisins. Spread over dough. Roll dough from long side and cut into 8 slices. Combine ⅓ C. brown sugar, honey and 2 T. butter and heat enough to dissolve sugar. Spoon 1 T. topping into 8 large, greased muffin pans. Place slides flat side down in muffin pans. Brush tops with remaining topping mixture. Bake in 400° oven 15 t0 20 minutes. Sprinkle with sunflower seeds. Makes 8 buns.

# Apple Streusel Muffins

2 C. flour (sifted)
½ C. sugar
3 tsp. baking powder
1 tsp. salt
½ C. butter
2 C. apples (chopped, peeled)

½ tsp. lemon rind (grated)
1 egg (beaten)
⅔ C. milk
¼ C. walnuts (chopped)
2 T. sugar
½ tsp. lemon rind (grated)

Sift together flour, ½ C. sugar, baking powder and salt into a large bowl. Cut in butter with a pastry blender until mixture is crumbly. Reserve ½ C. mixture for the streusel topping. Stir apple and ½ tsp. lemon rind into mixture in bowl. Add milk to egg and add to apple mixture; stir lightly until moist. Spoon into 12 greased muffin cups. Blend the ½ C. reserved mixture with walnuts, 2 T. sugar and ½ tsp. lemon rind. Sprinkle over batter in each muffin cup. Bake in 425° oven 20 minutes or until golden brown. Serve warm. Makes 12 muffins.

# Apple Cinnamon Oatmeal

1½ C. water
¼ tsp. salt
⅔ C. quick-cooking oatmeal
1 tsp. sugar

1 tsp. cinnamon
2 T. raisins
1 med. apple (peeled & grated)

Bring water and salt to boil in saucepan. Stir in oatmeal, apple, cinnamon and raisins. Reduce heat and cook 1 minute until water is absorbed. Serve hot.

# Apple Quick Bread

½ C. butter or margarine
C. sugar
eggs
tsp. vanilla
C. peeled apples (grated)
C. flour (sifted)
tsp. salt

1 tsp. baking powder
1 tsp. baking soda
1 tsp. cinnamon
½ tsp. cloves
¾ C. black walnuts (chopped)
1 T. lemon peel (grated)

Cream butter and sugar; add eggs and vanilla. Stir in apples. Sift together salt, flour, baking soda, baking powder and spices. Blend into creamed mixture; add nuts and lemon peel. Pour in 9x5x3-inch loaf pan. Bake 50 minutes at 350°. Cool in pan for 15 minutes.

# Spiced Applesauce Raisin Bread

¾ C. dry bran cereal
1¾ C. flour
½ C. sugar
½ C. brown sugar
1 C. applesauce
½ C. skim milk
¼ C. vegetable oil
3 tsp. baking powder

¾ tsp. cinnamon
½ tsp. allspice
½ tsp. salt
¼ tsp. cloves
1 egg or 2 egg whites or
   ¼ C. equivalent
½ C. raisins
Nuts (optional)

Grease bottom of loaf pan 9x5x3-inch. Crush cereal. Mix all ingredients except raisins; beat 30 seconds. Stir in raisins. Bake at 350° for 55 to 65 minutes or until toothpick in center comes out clean. Cool 10 minutes; remove from pan. Cool before slicing.

# Low Fat Apple-Cheddar Muffins

1³/₄ cups all-purpose flour
1 cup apples, cored, pared, and finely chopped
¹/₂ cup rye flour
¹/₄ cup reduced fat Cheddar cheese, shredded
¹/₂ cup chopped walnuts
¹/₄ sugar
2 tbsp. raisins
2 tsp. double-acting baking powder
¹/₈ tsp. ground nutmeg
¹/₈ tsp. cinnamon
¹/₂ cup skim milk
¹/₃ cup plus 2 tsp. reduced calorie margarine
¹/₄ cup frozen egg substitute, thawed

Preheat oven to 375 degrees. In medium mixing bowl combine first ten ingredients; stir to combine and set aside. In blender combine remaining ingredients and process until smooth. Pour into dry ingredients and stir until moistened (do not beat or over mix). Spray nonstick muffin tin with nonstick cooking spray; fill each cup with an equal amount of batter (each will be about 3/4 full). Bake in middle of center oven rack for 20 minutes (until muffins are golden brown and a toothpick inserted in center, comes out dry). Invert muffins onto wire rack and let cool. Yield 12 muffins

# Applesauce Honey Rolls

2 (1 lb.) loaves frozen bread dough
1 C. brown sugar (firmly packed)
¹/₂ C. honey
3 T. butter
4 T. butter (melted)
¹/₂ C. applesauce
2 T. brown sugar
¹/₄ C. raisins

Allow dough to thaw in plastic bag. Let rise until doubled in bulk. Mix brown sugar, honey and butter. Sprinkle mixture over the bottom of a 9x13-inch baking pan. Place dough on lightly floured pastry board or sheet and roll or pat into a 14x12-inch rectangle. Combine 4 T. butter, applesauce, 2 T. brown sugar and raisins; spread evenly over dough. Roll and seal. Cut into slices about ¹/₂ to 1-inch thick. Place slices on honey mixture in pan. Bake in 350° oven 30 minutes or until golden brown. Cool slightly and turn over onto a plate or tray. Makes 12 rolls.

# Applesauce Pecan Rolls

1 (13¾ oz.) pkg. roll mix
2 T. sugar
6 T. butter
1¾ C. applesauce

⅓ C. brown sugar (firmly packed)
½ C. pecans (chopped)
Cinnamon

Prepare roll mix according to directions on package; adding 2 T. sugar. Cover; let rise until doubled in bulk. Meanwhile, add 2 T. butter to applesauce; cook 10 minutes to evaporate some of the liquid, stirring occasionally. Melt remaining 4 T. butter in 9-inch baking pan; add brown sugar. Heat until dissolved. Roll out dough to 17x9-inch rectangle. Spread with cooled applesauce and sprinkle with pecans and cinnamon. Roll up jelly roll fashion. Cut in 1-inch slices. Arrange cut side up in pan on sugar mixture. Cover; let rise until doubled in bulk. Bake in 400° oven for 20 to 25 minutes or until golden brown. Serve hot. Makes 16 rolls.

# Apple Cinnamon Puffs

2 C. all-purpose flour
1 pkg. Red Star Active Dry Yeast
   or Quick-Rise Yeast
2 T. sugar
½ tsp. salt
¾ C. warm water

¼ C. oil
1 egg
1 C. apples (chopped)
3 T. butter (melted)
¼ C. sugar
1 tsp. cinnamon

In a large mixer bowl, combine 1 C. flour, yeast, 2 T. sugar and salt; mix well. Add very warm water (120°-130°) and oil to flour mixture. Add egg. blend at low speed until moistened; beat 3 minutes at medium speed. By hand, gradually stir in apples and remaining flour to make a soft batter. Spoon into well-greased muffin pan cups. Cover; let rise in warm place until double, about 1 hour (30 minutes for Quick-Rise Yeast). Bake at 375° for 15 to 20 minutes until golden brown. Makes 12 rolls. Combine ¼ C. sugar and cinnamon. Dip tops of hot rolls into melted butter, then into sugar-cinnamon mixture. Serve warm.

# Apple Pancakes

1/2 c. all-purpose, unbleached flour
1 T. sugar
1/2 tsp. salt
2 lg. eggs
2/3 c. half & half
1 tsp. vanilla extract
2 T. unsalted butter

4 lg. Granny Smith apples
1/4 c. packed light brown sugar
1/4 tsp. ground cinnamon
1 tsp. lemon juice
Maple syrup, lemon wedges &
    powdered sugar, for garnish

Preheat oven to 500°. Combine flour, sugar and salt in medium bowl. In second bowl, gently beat eggs. Add half & half and vanilla; stir to combine. Slowly add egg mixture to flour mixture and stir until smooth. Set aside.

Peel, core and quarter apples, then slice into thick slices. Melt butter in 10-inch nonstick, ovenproof skillet, on range until bubbly. Combine apples, brown sugar and cinnamon with butter in skillet on medium heat, stirring frequently, until apples are lightly browned. Remove from heat and stir in 1 teaspoon lemon juice. Pour batter around the edge of the apples, then over the top of the apples. Reduce oven heat to 425° and immediately place skillet in the oven. Bake for 17 to 20 minutes, until pancake is puffy, the edges of the pancake are slightly brown and have risen above the edge of the skillet.

Carefully remove hot skillet from oven with thick oven mitts, loosen edges of pancake from skillet, cut into four quarters and invert pancake quarters onto serving plates. Serve immediately. Drizzle with maple syrup, lemon juice or powdered sugar as desired. Yield: 4 servings.

**Hint:** Granny Smith or Braeburn apples work well in this recipe and should not be substituted for. Other apples will become too soft when sautéed or will not have enough flavor for this recipe.

# Apple Pancakes

1½ C. flour (sifted)
1½ tsp. baking powder
¾ tsp. salt
1 T. sugar

1 egg (beaten)
1¼ C. milk
2 T. oil
¾ C. peeled apples (grated)

Sift together flour, baking powder, salt and sugar. Combine egg, milk and oil. Add gradually to dry ingredients, stirring only until batter is smooth. Fold in apples. Drop by spoonfuls onto hot greased griddle. Cook slowly until the surface is covered with bubbles. Turn and cook until the bottom is a delicate brown. Makes about 18 medium-size pancakes.

# Baked Apple Pancake

Preheat oven to 425°.

2 apples, Granny Smith or other apple
   that will hold its shape
1/4 tsp. cinnamon

2 T. brown sugar
2 T. butter

Peel, quarter and core apples. Slice thin and sauté in butter for 5 minutes. Add cinnamon and brown sugar. Cover and cook approximate 10 minutes, or until they are tender but still hold their shape.

3 eggs
3/4 c. milk

3/4 c. flour
1 T. butter per baking dish

Place eggs in blender and blend for 1 minute. Add milk and flour. Blend 2 minutes longer, scraping sides of bowl.

Melt the butter in two (2-cup) ovenproof baking dishes in the preheated oven until the butter starts to brown. Spoon apples into the center of baking dish. Pour batter around the apples. Bake for 20 to 25 minutes. Yield: 2 servings.

# Applesauce Bran Muffins

1¼ C. flour
1 T. baking powder
¼ tsp. salt
2 C. any fibre cereal
1 C. skim milk

1 egg (slightly beaten)
½ C. chunky applesauce
⅓ C. brown sugar (packed)
2 tsp. margarine (melted)

Mix flour, baking powder and salt in a large bowl. Mix cereal and milk in another bowl; let stand 3 minutes. Stir in egg, applesauce, sugar and margarine. Add to dry ingredients; stir until just moistened. (Batter will be lumpy.) Spoon into sprayed or greased muffin pan ⅔ full. Bake 20 minutes in 400° oven. Makes 12. Serve warm. (140 calories; 2.5 g. fat.)

# Apple Cinnamon Muffins

¾ C. skim milk
⅓ C. non-fat plain yogurt
2 egg whites
1 egg
2 tsp. vanilla
Zest of one lemon
1½ C. all-purpose flour

⅓ C. dark brown sugar (firmly packed)
1½ tsp. ground cinnamon
1½ tsp. baking soda
¾ tsp. baking powder
1 med. apple (peeled, cored & chopped)

Heat oven to 375°. Spray only the bottoms of 12 medium muffin cups with PAM. In a large bowl, beat milk, yogurt, egg whites, eggs, vanilla and lemon zest. In a separate, bowl combine flour, sugar, cinnamon, baking soda and baking powder. Fold dry ingredients into wet until just moist. Stir in apple. Divide batter among muffin cups. Bake 18 to 20 minutes or until toothpick inserted into center comes out clean. Immediately remove from pan and cool on wire rack. Makes 1 dozen. (102 calories and 1 gram fat per muffin.)

# Sausage 'n Apple Muffins

2 cups flour
1 tbsp. firmly packed
    brown sugar
2½ tsp. baking powder
½ tsp. salt
¼ tsp. ground nutmeg
¾ cup shredded Swiss cheese
¼ cup dry white wine

⅓ cup vegetable oil
½ cup water
1 egg, lightly beaten
½ tsp. spicy brown mustard
⅔ pound bulk pork sausage,
    cooked, drained, cooled,
    and crumbled
¾ cup diced apple

Preheat oven to 375 degrees. In a large bowl stir together flour, brown sugar, baking powder, salt, and nutmeg. Stir in cheese to coat. In anoth bowl stir together wine, oil, water, egg, and mustard. Make a well in ce ter of dry ingredients; add wine mixture and stir just to combine. Stir i sausage and apple. Spoon batter into greased muffin tins. Bake 15 to 2 minutes or until a cake tester inserted in center of one muffin comes o clean. Remove muffin tins to wire rack. Cool 5 minutes before removi muffins from tins; finish cooling on rack. Serve warm or cool complete and store in airtight container in refrigerator. Let muffins reach room temperature or warm slightly before serving. Yield: 12 muffins

# Applesauce Bran Muffins

1 C. flour
2 tsp. baking powder
1/2 tsp. soda
1/2 tsp. cinnamon
2 C. bran cereal

1¼ C. 2% low-fat milk
⅓ C. brown sugar (packed)
1 egg
½ C. applesauce

Heat oven to 400°. Mix first 4 dry ingredients in bowl. Mix cereal, milk and brown sugar in another bowl; let stand 5 minutes. Stir in egg and applesauce. Add to flour mixture; stir until moistened. (Batter will be lumpy.) Spoon into muffin pans sprayed with no-stick cooking spray or paper liners.) Bake 18 to 20 minutes. Makes 12.

# Baked Apple French Toast

1/2 loaf French bread, sliced thick
8 eggs
3 c. milk
3/4 c. sugar, divided
1 T. vanilla

3 apples, cored, peeled & sliced
2 tsp. cinnamon
2 T. butter
Real maple syrup

Spray 9x13-inch baking dish lightly with cooking spray. Slice bread into 1.5-inch slices. Place bread tightly together in one layer in the baking dish. Place eggs in large bowl and beat lightly. Add milk, 1/4 cup sugar, vanilla and mix with whisk. Pour half of liquid over bread. Peel, core and slice apples. Cut into rings. Place rings on top of bread to cover. Pour remaining egg mixture over apples.

Mix remaining 1/2 cup sugar with cinnamon and sprinkle evenly over apples. Distribute small chunks of butter over the top. Bake for 30 minutes, or wrap and refrigerate overnight, baking at 400° for 50 minutes the next morning. Set 10 minutes before serving. Serve with real maple syrup. Yield: 8 to 12 servings, depending on serving size.

Recipe can be divided in half and baked in 9x9-inch pan for 20 to 30 minutes.

Garnish with powdered sugar, whipped cream and dried cranberries.

# Caramel Apple French Toast

3 or 4 cooking apples
1 tsp. cinnamon
Sugar, to taste (opt.)
3/4 c. packed brown sugar
3 T. light corn syrup
3 T. butter

3/4 c. walnuts or pecans, chopped
12 slices firm white bread
4 eggs, beaten
1 1/2 c. milk
1 tsp. vanilla
1/4 tsp. nutmeg (fresh if possible)

VANILLA SAUCE:
1/2 c. sugar
1 T. cornstarch

1 c. water
2 T. butter
1 T. vanilla

Peel, core and slice apples. Place in a medium-sized skillet. Pour 1/2 cup water over apples. Simmer 4 to 5 minutes until apples are softened. Drain apples in colander. Place in a bowl; gently mix in cinnamon and a little sugar if apples are tart. Set aside.

In the same skillet, combine brown sugar, corn syrup and butter. Cook and stir over medium heat until sugar melts and mixture just begins to become to a slow boil. Pour into a 9x13-inch baking dish. Sprinkle with nuts.

Place 6 slices of bread on top of syrup and nuts. Divide apples among bread slices and top with remaining 6 slices. Whisk together eggs, milk, vanilla and nutmeg. Pour over "apple sandwiches." Cover and refrigerate overnight.

In the morning, preheat oven to 325° and bake, uncovered, for 40 minutes. Remove from oven, cover with a serving platter, and invert. Cut each sandwich in half diagonally and serve with Vanilla Sauce.

**Vanilla Sauce:** Mix sugar, cornstarch and 1 cup water in a small saucepan. Cook, stirring often, over medium heat until thick and bubbly. Remove from heat, add butter and vanilla. Stir until butter melts.

# Mango Applesauce Waffles

1/2 c. flour
1 tsp. baking powder
3/4 c. quick oats
1 egg white, whipped

1/3 c. milk
1/4 c. canola oil
1/2 c. flavored applesauce
1 egg yolk

Preheat waffle iron. Mix dry ingredients. Blend liquid ingredients in 2 cups pouring cup. Fold dry mixture into the liquid. Fold in whipped egg white. Bake half of mixture in iron until steaming slows. Repeat for second waffle.

# Multi-Grain Pancakes

c. buckwheat pancake mix
c. biscuit mix
c. corn muffin mix
/2 c. All-Bran or Grape-Nuts cereal
/2 c. oatmeal

1 tsp. baking powder
1 tsp. cinnamon
1 Granny Smith apple, grated
2 eggs, beaten
2 c. low-fat milk

Preheat griddle. Mix all ingredients together in bowl, adding additional milk or water as needed to reach desired consistency for pancakes. Spray griddle with fat-free cooking spray and ladle mixture onto griddle using 1/4-cup measure. Cook until bubbles form and edges are set and turn once. Serve with syrup of choice.

Variation: Pumpkin may be substituted for apple.

Note: Recipe may be doubled or tripled as needed.

# Apple Muffins

2 cups whole wheat flour
1 tbsp. baking powder
1 tsp. cinnamon
2 egg whites or 1 egg

3/4 cup milk
1/4 cup honey
1/4 cup oil
1 cup apple, peeled and chopped

Mix dry ingredients. Combine egg, milk, honey, oil, and apples; mix well. Add wet ingredients to dry ingredients, stir. Bake at 375 degrees for 20 minutes.

# Apple, Cinnamon,
## and Raisin Muffins

2 cups flour
1 tbsp. baking powder
$^1/_2$ tsp. nutmeg
$^2/_3$ cup apple juice

$^1/_3$ cup oil
1 apple, grated
1 tsp. cinnamon
$^1/_2$ cup raisins

Combine all ingredients. Bake at 400 degrees for 15 to 20 minutes.

SERVING SUGGESTION: Make Cinnamon Crumble Topping – Mix 4 tbsp. sugar, 2 tbsp. flour, 1/2 tsp. cinnamon, and 1 tbsp. softened butter. Mix well by rubbing together with fingers. Sprinkle on muffir tops before baking.

# Double Apple Muffins

1½ cups flour
1 cup oatmeal
⅓ cup firmly packed
   brown sugar
1 tbsp. baking powder
1 tsp. cinnamon

½ tsp. salt
⅔ cup milk
⅓ cup apple juice
¼ cup vegetable oil
1 egg, beaten
¾ apple, peeled
   and chopped

Preheat oven to 400 degrees. Line 12 muffin tins with baking papers. Combine dry ingredients. Combine remaining ingredients. Stir together. Fill muffin tins 2/3 full. Bake 20 to 22 minutes. Makes 12 muffins at 160 calories each.

# Cookies

# Apple Cookies

1 C. butter
1 C. sugar
1 C. brown sugar (firmly packed)
2 eggs
1½ C. whole wheat flour
1½ C. flour (sifted)
1 tsp. salt
1 tsp. baking soda

1 tsp. ground cinnamon
¼ tsp. ground cloves
¼ tsp. ground allspice
1 C. peeled apple (grated)
1 C. granola
1 C. quick-cooking oats
1 C. raisins

Cream together butter and sugars until fluffy. Add eggs, one at a time, beating well. Combine flours, salt, baking soda, cinnamon, cloves and allspice. Add to creamed mixture; mix well. Add grated apple, cereal, oats and raisins. Drop by teaspoonfuls onto greased baking sheets. Bake in 350° oven about 15 minutes or until done. Makes about 6 dozen.

# Apple Oatmeal Cookies

1 C. shortening
1 C. brown sugar (firmly packed)
1 C. sugar
2 eggs
2 T. water
1 tsp. vanilla
1½ C. flour (sifted)

1 tsp. baking soda
1 tsp. salt
3 C. quick-cooking oats
1 C. chocolate or butterscotch chips
1 C. peeled apples (chopped)
½ C. nuts (chopped)

Cream together shortening and sugars. Add eggs, one at a time, beating well. Add water and vanilla. Sift together flour, baking soda and salt. Add to creamed mixture, mixing well. Add oats, chips, apples and nuts. Drop by teaspoonfuls onto greased baking sheet. Bake in 375° oven 10 to 12 minutes or until done. Makes about 8 dozen.

# Apple Butter Cookies

¼ C. sugar
½ C. butter
1 C. apple butter
1 tsp. baking soda
2 C. flour
½ tsp. salt

1 tsp. baking powder
½ C. buttermilk
½ tsp. vanilla
½ C. raisins
½ C. nuts

Cream sugar and butter. Mix apple butter and soda; add to mixture. Sift together flour, salt, baking powder; add alternately with milk and vanilla to ixture. Mix thoroughly. Stir in raisins and nuts. Bake in 350° oven 10 to 12 minutes on greased cookie sheet.

# Cheesy Apple Cookies

¾ C. sugar
½ C. butter
1 egg
1 tsp. vanilla
¾ C. sifted flour
½ tsp. baking powder

½ tsp. cinnamon
1½ C. oatmeal
1½ C. shredded cheese
1½ C. tart apples, finely chopped
1 tsp. salt

Cream sugar, butter, eggs and vanilla. Sift flour, baking powder, salt, cinnamon and add to creamed mixture. Stir in remaining ingredients. Drop by teaspoonfuls onto ungreased cookie sheet. Bake at 350° for 12 to 15 minutes or until golden brown. Makes 4 dozen cookies.

# Apple Oatmeal Cookies

1 1/2 c. whole wheat blend or
   enriched all-purpose flour
2 tsp. baking powder
1/2 tsp. salt
1/2 tsp. cinnamon
2 c. old-fashioned oatmeal

1 c. finely-chopped apples
1/4 c. tub margarine
1/4 c. brown sugar
Egg substitute to = 2 eggs
1/4 c. apple juice concentrate,
   thawed

Blend together flour, baking powder, salt and cinnamon. Stir in oats and apples; set aside. In a large mixing bowl, cream margarine and sugar until fluffy. Add egg substitute, 1/4 cup at a time. Stir into flour mixture alternately with apple juice concentrate. Drop by teaspoon onto a cookie sheet, that has been sprayed with cooking spray. Bake in 375° preheated oven 12 to 15 minutes, or until golden brown. Cool on waxed paper.
**Yield: 36 cookies**

# Applesauce Brownies

1 C. margarine
2 C. sugar
4 eggs
1 C. applesauce
2 tsp. vanilla
2 C. flour

4 T. cocoa
1 tsp. baking powder
½ tsp. soda
½ tsp. salt
1 C. nuts (chopped)

Cream shortening and sugar until fluffy. Add eggs, applesauce and vanilla; beat well. Add sifted dry ingredientrs and mix until blended. Stir in nuts and spread in jelly roll pan. Bake at 350° for 30 minutes. Frosting is optional.

# Pies

# Cheese Apple Pie

Pastry for 9-inch two-crust pie
¾ C. granulated sugar
2 T. flour
⅛ tsp. salt
5 C. sliced, pared, cored apples

1 C. grated process sharp
   Cheddar cheese
2 tsp. lemon juice
3 T. heavy cream

Preheat oven to 425°. Line 9-inch pie plate with pastry; roll out top crust. Combine sugar, flour, salt, and ⅔ C. cheese. Sprinkle half of mixture in lined pie plate; heap apples on top and sprinkle with lemon juice. Cover with rest of sugar mixture, ⅓ C. cheese, and cream; adjust top crust. Bake for 45 minutes or until apples are tender. Serve warm.

# Mom's Apple Pie

5½ to 6 C. peeled, cored &
   sliced tart cooking apples
1 C. sugar
2 T. flour
½ tsp. cinnamon
1 tsp. vanilla

2 drops coconut flavoring
⅔ C. Half & Half
2 to 3 T. lemon juice to
   keep apples from darkening
2 to 3 T. butter
2 pie crusts

Combine all ingredients in a bowl and mix together thoroughly. Preheat oven to 450°. Roll out pie dough for bottom layer of crust and fit into 9-inch pan. Fill with apple filling and dot with butter. Roll out dough for top crust and fit to top of pie. Make design in top crust. Brush top of unbaked pie with milk or cream and sprinkle with sugar and cinnamon mixture. Bake at 450° for 10 minutes. Reduce oven to 350° and bake another 30 to 40 minutes, until crust is golden brown and apples feel tender. Cool on rack. Serves 8.

# Do It's Own Crust

# French Apple Pie

6 C. sliced pared tart apples
1¼ tsp. ground cinnamon
¼ tsp. ground nutmeg
1 C. sugar

¾ C. milk
½ C. Bisquick baking mix
2 eggs
2 T. margarine or butter (softened)
Streusel (below)

Heat oven to 325°. Grease pie plate, 10x1½-inches. Mix apples and spices; turn into plate. Beat remaining ingredients, except Streusel until smooth, 15 seconds in blender on high or 1 minute with hand beater. Pour into plate. Sprinkle with Streusel. Bake until knife inserted in center comes out clean, 55 to 60 minutes.

For Streusel: Mix 1 C. Bisquick baking mix, ½ C. chopped nuts, ⅓ C. packed brown sugar, and 3 T. firm margarine or butter until crumbly.

# Apple Pie

6 C. sliced tart juicy apples
¾ C. sugar

¾ tsp. cinnamon
1 T. butter

Preheat oven to 425°. Combine apples, sugar and spice. Heap into pastry lined pie pan; dot with butter. Cover with top crust. Seal and flute edges. Bake at 425° for 50-60 minutes until done.

# Luscious Apple Pie

6 large tart apples
1 C. sugar (½ brown & ½ white)
¾ tsp. cinnamon
¼ tsp. nutmeg
1 T. lemon juice

1 T. flour
⅛ tsp. ginger
⅛ tsp. salt
3 T. butter

Peel apples and slice paper thin. Food processor works good. Combine remaining ingredients and toss gently with apples, except butter. Put apple mixture into pie shell. Dot with butter. Place top crust and cut vents. Bake at 400° for 10 minutes. Reduce to 350° and bake for 45 minutes longer. Non-convention oven, bake at 375° for about 50 minutes.

CRUST:
2 C. flour
1 tsp. salt

⅔ C. lard
6 T. cold water

Cut lard in flour and salt. When mealy looking, add just enough water to moisten. Roll out. Makes two 9-inch crusts. Dust top with milky sugar before baking.

# Green Apple Pie

4 C. green apples (peeled & sliced)
1 C. sugar
½ tsp. cinnamon

¼ tsp. nutmeg
Lemon juice (few drops)
Butter

Place peeled and sliced green apples in unbaked pie shell. Add sugar, nutmeg, a few drop of lemon juice and a few dabs of butter. Place unbaked top crust on and bake in moderate oven.

# Apple Betty Pie

4 C. sliced pared tart apples
¼ C. orange juice
1 C. sugar
¾ C. flour

½ tsp. cinnamon
¼ tsp. nutmeg
½ C. butter

Mound apples in buttered 9-inch pie plate and sprinkle with orange juice.

For Topping: Combine sugar, flour, spices, and dash of salt. Cut in butter until mixture is crumbly, then scatter over apples. Bake at 375° for 45 minutes or until apples are done and topping is crisp. Serve warm with cream or ice cream.

# Apple Crumb Pie

4 large tart apples
1 unbaked pastry shell
1 C. sugar

1 tsp. cinnamon
¾ C. flour (scant)
⅓ C. butter

Peel apples, slice, and arrange in unbaked pastry shell. Sprinkle with ½ C. sugar, mixed with cinnamon. Sift remaining ½ C. sugar with flour. Cut butter into sugar and flour until very crumbly. Sprinkle over apples. Bake in hot oven at 450° about 10 minutes. Reduce heat to 350° and bake for 30 minutes, until apples are tender.

# Fresh Apple and Banana Pie

1 (9") unbaked margarine
  low-fat pie shell
6 c. apples, peeled, cored
  & thinly sliced
2 med. bananas, peeled &
  sliced thick

1/2 c. sugar or equivalent
  sweetener
1/2 c. all-purpose
  enriched flour
1/2 tsp. cinnamon
1/2 tsp. cardamom
2 T. lemon juice

TOPPING:
1/4 c. enriched all-purpose
  flour
1/2 c. brown sugar

1/2 tsp. ground cinnamon
3 T. tub margarine
1/4 c. rolled oats

In a large bowl, combine apples, bananas, sugar, flour, cinnamon, cardamom and lemon juice. Toss to blend. Pour into unbaked pie shell. Combine topping ingredients and sprinkle over top. Bake in a 425° preheated oven for 40 to 50 minutes. Cover top once crust browns.
**Yield: 8 servings**

# Apple Pie Surprise

Egg substitute to equal
  1 egg
2/3 c. sugar or equivalent
  sweetener
1/2 c. enriched all-purpose
  flour

1/2 tsp. baking powder
1/4 tsp. salt (opt.)
1 c. apples, peeled, cored
  & diced
1/2 c. raisins

Mix egg substitute and sugar thoroughly. Add remaining ingredients. Spray a 9-inch pie pan with vegetable oil. Pour apple batter into pie plate and distribute evenly. Bake in a 350° preheated oven for 30 minutes.
  Good served hot with skim milk poured over it.
**Yield: 6 servings**

# Sour Cream Apple Pie

¾ C. sugar
2 T. all-purpose flour
1 (8 oz.) carton sour cream
1 egg
1 tsp. vanilla

¼ tsp. ground nutmeg
1/8 tsp. salt
4 C. apples (pared, cored,
     and sliced)
1 unbaked 9-inch pie shell

STRUESEL TOPPING:
¾ C. all-purpose flour
¼ C. sugar
¾ tsp. cinnamon

¼ C. butter or margarine
¼ C. nuts (chopped)

In a large bowl, combine sugar and flour. Blend in sour cream, egg, vanilla, nutmeg and salt until smooth. Fold in apple slices. Pour mixture into pie shell. If desired, to prevent over-browning, cover edge of pastry with foil. Remove when struesel topping is added. Bake in 400° oven for 15 minutes. Reduce oven temperature to 350°. Continue baking for 25 minutes. Sprinkle with struesel topping. Continue baking for 10 to 15 minutes or until pie is set and topping begins to brown. Makes 6 to 8 servings.

For Struesel Topping: In small bowl, combine flour, sugar and cinnamon. Cut in butter or margarine until crumbly. Stir in nuts.

# Cranberry Apple Pie

3 C. sliced apples (such as
     Jonathan, Romes, Laura Red)
1 (16 oz.) can whole cranberry
     sauce
¾ C. walnuts

¼ C. sugar
¼ C. flour
1 tsp. cinnamon
2 deep dish pie crusts (frozen
     or homemade)

Combine filling ingredients in large bowl; mix. Pour 1 pie crust. Cut the crimp off remaining pie crust. Place upright on filled crust. Let thaw 10 to 12 minutes. Crimp edges together. Cut 2 to 3 slits in top crust. Place in preheated oven 375°. Bake 40 to 45 minutes or until lightly brown and apples are soft when pierced by a fork. Serve warm or cool with ice cream or a cheese wedge.

# Blue Cheese Apple Pie

PASTRY:

1 C. flour
¼ tsp. salt
¼ C. butter/oleo (½ stick)

⅓ C. blue cheese (crumbled)
3-4 T. cold water

FILLING:

6 C. (7 or 8) peeled apples (sliced)
½ C. raisins
½ C. sugar

⅓ C. water
2 T. cornstarch
2 T. water

TOPPING:

1 C. dairy sour cream
2 tsp. lemon juice

2 tsp. sugar
¼ tsp. cinnamon

Mix pastry ingredients as for pie crust. Bake in 9-inch pie pan for 12 to 15 minutes. Combine filling ingredients, except water and cornstarch, in 3 qt. saucepan. Cook until apples are tender. Add cornstarch, dissolved in water and cook until smooth, stirring. Boil 2 minutes. Spoon into baked pie shell. Combine topping ingredients and spoon over apples. Bake at 425° for 4 to 5 minutes or until topping is set.

# Red Hot Apple Pie

1 plain pie crust recipe

Syrup:

¾ c. sugar
½ c. water
¼ c. red hot candies

6 med. tart apples, peeled & sliced

1 T. lemon juice
1-2 T. flour

Cook the candies, sugar, water and lemon juice until candies are melted. Add the apples and stir till they are all red. Drain off the juice and save. Put the apples in the pie crust. Add a little flour to the juice. Pour over the apples in the crust. Dot with butter. Put on the top crust. Bake at 400° for 50 minutes.

# Vermont Apple Pie

Pastry for 9-inch double crust pie
6-8 apples (peeled & sliced)
1 T. lemon juice
¾ C. brown sugar
2 T. flour

1 tsp. cinnamon
½ tsp. nutmeg
¼ tsp. allspice
¼ C. maple syrup
1 T. butter or oleo

Preheat oven to 425°. Line pie pan with pastry. Toss apple slices with lemon juices, drain and arrange in pastry line pan. Combine brown sugar, flour and spices. Sprinkle over apples. Drizzle with maple syrup and dot with butter. Top with remaining pastry. Bake 10 minutes, reduce heat to 350° for 45 minutes or until apples are tender to crust brown. Cover edges of crust with foil if needed.

# Caramel Apple Pie

Pastry for 2-crust pie
6-8 tart apples, pared, cored, sliced
¼ c. granulated sugar
2 T. flour

1 tsp. cinnamon
¼ tsp. salt
2 T. butter
⅓ c. dark corn syrup

Topping:

¼ c. brown sugar
2 T. butter
2 T. flour

¼ c. dark syrup
¼ c. nuts

Arrange apples in pastry-lined 8-inch pie plate. Combine granulated sugar, 2 tablespoons flour, cinnamon, salt, 2 tablespoons butter, ⅓ cup dark syrup; pour over apples. Adjust top crust, cutting slits for escape of steam; seal. Bake in hot oven (425°) for 40 minutes or until crust is browned and apples are tender. Remove from oven. Combine remaining ingredients except nuts; spread over pie; sprinkle with nuts. Return pit to oven for 5 minutes or till topping is bubbly.

98

# Macaroon Topped Apple Pie

6 med.-sized apples (peeled & sliced)
1 C. sugar (divided)
½ tsp. cinnamon
1 egg (beaten)
½ tsp. baking powder
1 tsp. salt
½ C. flour
½ tsp. vanilla
½ C. sweetened coconut
2 T. butter

In a medium-sized bowl, stir apples with ½ C. sugar and cinnamon, enough to coat apples. Pour mixture into a buttered 9-inch pie pan. Bake in 375° oven for 20 minutes. Meanwhile, prepare topping by creaming butter with ½ C. sugar. Add egg, sifted dry ingredients, vanilla and coconut. Spread mixture evenly over hot apples. Bake at 375° for 30 minutes or until apples are tender and crust is golden brown. Serve warm or cold. NOTE: If using a glass pie plate, lower oven temperature to 350°. Serves 8. Garnish with unpeeled apple slices, ice cream, or wedge of cheese.

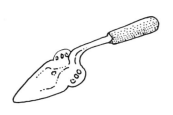

# Cranberry Apple Pie

1 C. cranberries
3 C. peeled apples (sliced)
1 C. sugar
2 T. flour
1/8 tsp. salt
2 T. butter
PASTRY:
2 C. flour
1 tsp. salt
⅔ C. shortening
1 tsp. orange peel (grated)
⅓ C. orange juice

Prepare orange pastry for double 9-inch pie. Combine cranberries, apples, sugar, flour and salt; mix well. Turn into pastry-lined pie pan. Cover with top crust. Cut vents in top. Flute edges. Bake in 400° oven 50 minutes or until apples are tender. Makes 6 to 8 servings.

# Apple Custard Pie

2 all-purpose apples (pared & sliced)
1 T. ReaLemon lemon juice from concentrate
10 T. biscuit baking mix
1 (14 oz.) can Eagle Brand sweetened condensed milk (NOT evaporated milk)

1½ C. water
3 eggs
¼ C. margarine or butter (softened)
1½ tsp. vanilla extract
½ tsp. EACH ground cinnamon & nutmeg

CRUMB TOPPING:
½ C. EACH biscuit baking mix & brown sugar (packed)

½ C. EACH cold margarine & nuts (chopped)

Toss apples with ReaLemon brand then 2 T. biscuit mix; arrange in buttered 10-inch pie plate. In blender, combine remaining ingredients. Blend on low 3 minutes; let stand 5 minutes. Pour over apples; top with Crumb Topping. Bake at 350° for 35 minutes or until golden. Cool

For Crumb Topping: Combine biscuit baking mix and brown sugar; mix in margarine and nuts.

# Cakes

# Apple Cake

4 c. sliced apples (Granny Smith)
2 c. sugar
1/2 c. canola oil
2 eggs, beaten
2 tsp. vanilla
1 c. raisins

1/2 c. chopped walnuts
2 c. flour
1/2 tsp. salt
2 tsp. baking soda
2 tsp. cinnamon

TOPPING:
2 T. flour
1/2 c. milk

1/2 c. butter
1/2 c. sugar
1 tsp. vanilla

Sift all dry ingredients together in a bowl. In a separate bowl, whisk eggs, vanilla and oil together; set aside.

In a large bowl, combine sliced, peeled apples, sugar, raisins and nuts; toss to coat. Add the egg mixture. Then add the dry ingredients and mix thoroughly. Spread in a greased and floured 9x13-inch pan. Bake at 350° for 45 minutes to 1 hour, until tests done with toothpick. Cool.

**Topping:** In a small saucepan, cook flour with milk. Stir until thickened (like for a white sauce). Cool thoroughly. Mixture must be cooled or it will not blend properly. Mix until fluffy softened butter and sugar. Add two mixtures together and add vanilla. Spread on top of cake

# Down Home Apple Cake

¼ C. shortening
1 C. sugar
1 egg
4 C. apples (chopped)
1 C. unsifted flour

1 tsp. baking soda
1/8 tsp. salt
1 tsp. cinnamon
½ tsp. nutmeg

Cream shortening and sugar. Mix in egg and apples. Sift rest of ingredients; add to apple mixture. Batter is thick. Spread in greased 9-inch square baking pan. Bake at 325° for 45 minutes. While warm, cut into squares. Sprinkle with powdered sugar.

# Apple Cake

2 C. sugar
2½ C. self-rising flour
1 C. oil
4-5 med. apples (sliced)

1 tsp. cinnamon
2 eggs
1 tsp. vanilla
1 C. nuts/raisins (optional)

ICING:
½ stick butter
2 oz. cream cheese
2 C. powdered sugar

1 tsp. vanilla
1-2 T. milk
Nuts (optional)

Mix cake ingredients. Batter will be thick. Pour in greased 9x13-inch pan. Bake at 350° for 55 to 60 minutes. Cool and frost. (1 C. regular flour plus 1½ tsp. baking powder and ½ tsp. salt equals 1 C. self raising flour.)

# Apple Cake

1 c. sugar
½ c. butter
1 egg
Dash of salt
½ c. cold coffee

½ c. chopped raw apples
1½ c. flour
1 tsp. soda
1 tsp. vanilla

Topping:

½ c. brown sugar
½ c. nuts, chopped

1 tsp. cinnamon

Beat butter and sugar until mixed well, add the egg and salt. Mix in the cold coffee. Mix the flour and soda and mix into the butter mixture. Add the vanilla and apples. Mix well and put in a 9 x 13-inch pan. Mix the brown sugar, nuts and cinnamon and sprinkle over the apple mixture in pan and bake in a 325° oven for 45 minutes to 1 hour. This is good served with whip cream or ice cream. It is also very good like it is.

# Applesauce Chocolate Cake

½ C. shortening
¾ tsp. salt
½ tsp. cinnamon
½ tsp. cloves
½ tsp. nutmeg
½ tsp. allspice
2 T. cocoa
1½ C. sugar

2 eggs
1½ tsp. baking soda
2 C. flour (sifted)
¾ C. nutmeats
¾ C. dates (chopped)
¾ C. raisins (chopped)
1½ C. unsweetened applesauce

Blend shortening, spices and cocoa. Add sugar gradually, then eggs. Beat well. Add soda to flour and sift 3 times. Flour the fruits with 2 T. of flour. Add dry ingredients alternately with applesauce. Pour into 9-inch square cake pan. Bake at 350° for 55 to 60 minutes.

# Applesauce Cake

1 C. butter (room temperature)
1 C. sugar
2 eggs
3½ C. sifted all-purpose flour
1 tsp. baking soda
Pinch of salt

1 tsp. cinnamon
2 tsp. cloves
2 tsp. nutmeg
1 C. walnuts (chopped)
2 C. raisins
2 C. unsweetened applesauce

Cream butter and sugar together until light and fluffy. Add eggs; beat well. Set aside. Sift together flour, baking soda, salt and spices. Remove ½ C. of flour mixture and stir into nuts and raisins. Set both aside. Alternately stir flour mixture and applesauce into creamed mixture. Mix well. Add nuts and raisins; stir to blend. Pour batter into greased and floured bundt cake pan. Bake at 350° for 65 to 75 minutes, or until cake tests done when wooden pick is inserted near center. Cool in pan 10 minutes; turn out on rack to complete cooling. Yield: 20 to 24 servings.

# Raisin Apple Coffee Cake

¾ C. sugar
¼ C. shortening
1 egg
1½ C. flour

2 tsp. baking powder
½ tsp. salt
1 tsp. vanilla
½ C. raisins

TOPPING:
2 apples (peeled & sliced)
1 tsp. cinnamon

½ C. raisins
2 T. sugar

Cream sugar and shortening; add egg and dry ingredients. Mix well. Pour into greased 9-inch square pan. Arrange apple slices on top of batter. Sprinkle with cinnamon and sugar mixture. Bake at 375° for 25 to 35 minutes.

# Apple Cake with Caramel Topping

¼ C. butter or margarine
1 C. sugar
1 egg
1 C. all-purpose flour
1 tsp. baking soda

1 tsp. ground nutmeg
½ tsp. ground cinnamon
2 C. apples (diced)
½ C. nuts (chopped)
Caramel sauce

CARAMEL SAUCE:
½ C. butter or margarine
½ C. brown sugar (packed)
½ C. sugar

½ C. heavy cream
1 T. vanilla

In a small mixer bowl, cream butter or margarine and sugar until fluffy. Add egg; beat well. In a small bowl, combine flour, baking soda, nutmeg and cinnamon. Add to creamed mixture. Beat just until combined. By hand, fold in apples and nuts. Spread batter in a greased 8x8x2-inch baking pan. Bake in a 350° oven for 35 to 45 minutes or until done. Serve warm with caramel sauce. Makes 9 servings.

For Caramel Sauce: In a small saucepan, melt butter or margarine. Stir in brown sugar, sugar and heavy cream. Bring just to boiling over medium heat, stirring constantly. Remove from heat and stir in vanilla. Serve over warm cake. Makes about 1½ C. sauce.

# Apple Coffee Cake

3 med. size apples
½ lemon
1 tsp. cinnamon
1 C. butter
2 C. sugar
4 large eggs
1 C. sour cream

1 T. vanilla
2½ C. flour
1 tsp. baking powder
1 tsp. baking soda
1 T. cinnamon
½ C. brown sugar
1 C. pecans (chopped)

Peel, core and chop apples into small pieces. Place in a large bowl and toss with lemon juice and 1 tsp. cinnamon. Cream butter and sugar; beat in eggs, sour cream and vanilla. Sift flour, baking powder and baking soda together. Fold into the sour cream mixture. Stir in the chopped apples and pour ½ of this batter in a 10-inch tube pan. In small bowl, mix remaining 1 T. cinnamon, brown sugar and chopped pecans together. Sprinkle over the batter in pan. Add the rest of the batter and smooth the top. Bake 1⅓ hours in 350° oven. Remove from oven and cool at least 10 minutes before removing from pan.

# Apple Upside Down Cake

¼ C. butter
¾ C. brown sugar

Thick apple rings (enough to cover pan)

Melt butter in pan; add brown sugar. Arrange apple rings over butter-sugar mixture. Cover with gingerbread or plain cake batter and bake.

# Apple-Yogurt Coffee Cake

⅔ C. sugar
½ C. butter or margarine
2 eggs
1 tsp. vanilla
1¼ C. ground rolled oats (start
  with 1⅔ C. oats & grind in
  blender or food processor)
1 C. all-purpose flour

1 tsp. baking powder
1 tsp. baking soda
1 (8 oz.) carton plain yogurt
2 C. peeled cooking apples
  (finely chopped)
½ C. nuts (chopped)
½ C. brown sugar (packed)
1 T. butter or margarine (melted)

In a large mixing bowl, beat together the sugar and butter or margarine until fluffy. Add the eggs and vanilla; beat well. Combine oats, flour, baking powder and baking soda. Add to beaten mixture alternately with yogurt, beating after each addition until the mixture is just combined. Fold in the apples. Divide batter between two greased and floured 8x1½-inch round baking pans. Combine the nuts, brown sugar or margarine. Sprinkle over the butter in pans. Bake in a 350° oven for 30 to 35 minutes or until done. Cool coffee cakes in pans on wire racks. Serve warm or cooled. Makes 2 coffee cakes, 6 to 8 servings each.

# Apple Filling

2 lg. apples, grated
1 lemon, juice & grated
  rind

1 c. sugar
Egg substitute to = 1 egg

Pare 2 large apples and grate into a saucepan. Add lemon juice and grated rind. Add sugar and egg substitute. Bring to a boil very slowly, but DO NOT BOIL. Cool before spreading on cake.
**Yield: enough for a 9x13-inch cake; serving 24.**

# Holiday Apple Cake

| | |
|---|---|
| 4 c. unpeeled cooking apples, finely chopped | 1/4 c. skim milk |
| 1/2 c. orange juice, divided | 3 c. flour |
| 1 1/2 tsp. cinnamon | 2 tsp. baking powder |
| 1 c. sugar | 1/4 tsp. salt |
| 1/2 c. margarine, softened | 2 1/2 tsp. vanilla |
| 1 (8 oz.) ctn. egg sub- stitute, thawed | 2 T. brown sugar |
| | 2 T. oatmeal, dry |
| | Nonstick vegetable cooking spray |

1. Combine apples, 1/4 cup orange juice and cinnamon in a bowl; stir well and set aside.
2. Cream sugar and margarine at medium speed with an electric mixer until light and fluffy, about 5 minutes.
3. Add egg substitute; beat 4 minutes at medium speed or until well blended.
4. Combine remaining 1/4 cup orange juice and milk; set aside.
5. Combine flour, baking powder and salt.
6. With mixer on low speed, add to creamed mixture alternately with milk mixture, beginning and ending with flour mixture; stir in vanilla.
7. Pour half of batter into a 10-inch tube pan coated with cooking spray; top with half of apple mixture.
8. Pour remaining batter into pan; top with remaining apple mixture, and sprinkle with brown sugar and oatmeal.
9. Bake at 350°F. for 1 hour and 10 minutes or until a wooden pick inserted in center comes out clean.
10. Cool in pan 10 minutes; remove from pan, and cool on a wire rack.

**Yield: 16 servings**

# Apple Crisp Cake

1/3 c. oatmeal
3 T. brown sugar
1 T. flour
1 T. tub margarine, melted
1/3 c. unsweetened apple juice
  concentrate, thawed

4 c. Granny Smith apples,
  peeled, cored & sliced
1/2 tsp. cinnamon
1/4 tsp. cardamom

In a small bowl, blend oatmeal, sugar and flour. Cut in margarine. Add 1 tablespoon apple juice concentrate, tossing with fork to blend. Set aside. In a second bowl, put sliced apples, cinnamon and cardamom. Blend well. Add remaining apple juice concentrate, blending well. Pour into an 8-inch square baking dish, that has been sprayed with cooking spray. Sprinkle with oatmeal mixture. Bake in 400° preheated oven for 25 to 30 minutes.

Yield: 6 servings

# Apple-Crumb Coffee Cake

3 c. Master Baking Mix
  (see index)
1/3 c. sugar or equivalent
  sweetener
Egg substitute to equal
  1 egg
1 c. water
1 tsp. vanilla
1/2 tsp. almond extract
  (opt.)
1 1/2 c. chopped apples
  (peeled & cored)

1/2 c. raisins (plumped in
  1 c. boiling water for
  15 minutes, drained)
1/3 c. all-purpose flour
1/2 c. dry bread crumbs
1/2 c. brown sugar, firmly
  packed
1 tsp. cinnamon
1/2 tsp. cardamom
3 T. tub margarine

In a large mixing bowl, combine Master Baking Mix and sugar; set aside. In a small bowl, combine egg substitute, water, vanilla and almond extract. Fold into dry ingredients, stirring until well blended. Pour into an 8-inch square pan that has been sprayed with vegetable oil. Sprinkle chopped apples and raisins over top. Mix together flour, bread crumbs, brown sugar, cinnamon, cardamom and margarine until mixture is crumbly. Mix with pastry blender or fingers. Sprinkle mixture over apple-raisins mixture. Bake in a 350° preheated oven for 40 to 50 minutes, or until done.

Yield: 9 servings

# Apple Nut Cake

1 C. cooking oil
2 C. sugar
3 eggs
2 tsp. vanilla
3 C. flour

1 tsp. soda
1 tsp. salt
3 C. diced apples
1 C. chopped nuts

Mix together oil, sugar, eggs, and vanilla. Add flour, soda, salt, apples, and nuts. Bake at 350° for 1 hour in angel food cake pan. Remove from pan when cool.

TOPPING FOR APPLE NUT CAKE:

1 stick oleo
1 C. brown sugar

¼ C. milk

Cook for 3 to 4 minutes and pour over cake.

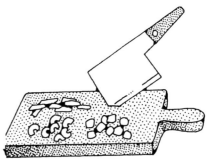

# Grandma's Apple Cake

1 stick butter or margarine
½ C. sugar
2-3 eggs
Salt
1¾ C. flour

2 tsp. baking powder
1-4 T. milk
Lemon flavoring (optional)
1-2 apples

Smooth butter and add slowly the sugar, eggs, and spices. Mix flour and baking powder; add tablespoon by tablespoon to the mixture. If dough is too stif, add milk. Put in greased baking tin and level. Peel apple, quarter it and cut apple quarter, not through horizontal and vertical and put them on the dough. Bake at 325° for 40 to 50 minutes. Sieve powdered sugar on the cold cake.

111

# Family Apple Cake

4 C. chopped apples
2 C. sugar
2 beaten eggs
2 C all-purpose flour
2 tsp. baking soda
3 tsp. cinnamon
1 tsp. salt
Nuts (optional)

1 C. brown sugar
1 C. granulated sugar
6 T. all-purpose flour
2 C. water
½ C. margarine or butter
1 tsp. vanilla
Nuts

Mix apples and 2 C. sugar and let stand for 1 hour or longer. Add eggs, 2 C flour, soda, cinnamon, salt, and nuts. Mix and put into 9x13-inch greased pan. Bake at 350° for 45 minutes.

For Topping: During last 15 to 20 minutes of baking time, mix together brown sugar, granulated sugar, 6 T. flour, and water. Bring to a boil, stirring often. Turn down heat and simmer for 15 minutes. Remove from heat and add butter, vanilla, and nuts. Pour over the cake while hot. Serve warm or cold.

# Chunky Apple Cake

1 can apple pie mix
1 C. sugar
½ C. softened butter or margarine
2 eggs
2 tsp. vanilla

2 tsp. cinnamon
1 tsp. salt
½ C. walnuts
2 tsp. baking soda
2 C. flour

Mix by hand in a large bowl the pie mix, sugar, butter, eggs, vanilla, cinnamon, salt, walnuts, and baking soda. Mix well and add flour. Pour into 9x13-inch pan and bake at 350° for 50 minutes.

# Mom's Applesauce Cake

½ C. shortening
1 C. sugar
2 eggs (beaten)
1½ C. sweetened applesauce
2 C. all-purpose flour
1 tsp. baking soda

½ tsp. salt
1 tsp. cinnamon
½ tsp. cloves
½ tsp. nutmeg
1 C. raisins
1 tsp. vanilla

Cream shortening and sugar together. Add beaten eggs. Add applesauce and vanilla. Sift together flour, soda, salt, cinnamon, cloves, and nutmeg. Add to applesauce mixture. Put into a greased 9x13-inch pan. Bake at 350° for 40 to 45 minutes.

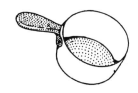

# Apple Bundt Cake

2 eggs
2 C. sugar
½ C. oil
2 tsp. baking soda
½ tsp. salt
1 C. nuts (chopped)

2 C. all-purpose flour (sifted)
1 tsp. cinnamon
4 C. peeled & diced apples
½ C. chopped nuts
½ tsp. vanilla

Beat eggs; add sugar and mix well. Add oil and sifted dry ingredients and blend thoroughly. Stir in diced apples, nuts, and vanilla. Batter will be very thick. Spoon into a greased and floured bundt pan. Bake at 350° for 1 hour. Cool in pan for 10 to 15 minutes. Turn onto plate. You may drizzle powdered sugar frosting over it when removed from pan. This is a very moist, delicious cake. It could also be served with Cool Whip or ice cream.

# One Pan Applesauce Cake

2 C. Bisquick baking mix
1 C. applesauce or
   1 C. chopped apples
½ C. packed brown sugar
¼ C. vegetable oil
½ tsp. ground cinnamon

¼ tsp. ground cloves
¼ tsp. ground allspice
2 eggs
½ C. raisins
½ C. chopped nuts
Ice cream

Heat oven to 350°. Mix all ingredients, except raisins, nuts, and ice cream in ungreased square pan, 9x9x2-inch or 8x8x2-inches with fork until moistened. Stir vigorously until well blended; stir in raisins and nuts. Bake until wooden pick inserted in center comes out clean, 35 to 40 minutes. Serve warm or cool with ice cream.

# Applesauce Cake

2 C. brown sugar
1 C. butter
2½ C. flour
2 C. apple sauce
1 C. raisins
1 C. nutmeat (your choice)

1 tsp. soda
1 tsp. cinnamon
1 tsp. allspice
1 tsp. nutmeg
¼ tsp. salt

Cream butter and sugar together. Add apple sauce, raisins and nut meats. Sift flour, soda and spices together and add to mixture. Gradually beat after each addition. Bake in 375° oven for 30 minutes.

# Applesauce Gingerbread

1/3 cup butter
½ cup brown sugar
½ cup molasses
1 egg
1¾ cup all-purpose flour or
   2 cups cake flour
½ teaspoon salt

1 teaspoon baking powder
½ teaspoon soda
1½ teaspoons ginger
1 teaspoon cinnamon
2 cups sliced apples
¾ cup sour milk or buttermilk

Cream butter and add sugar.

Beat until fluffy.

Add beaten egg and molasses and continue to beat until thoroughly blended.

Sift flour; measure and add salt, soda and baking powder. Sift again.

Add dry ingredients alternately with sour milk.

Beat thoroughly after each addition.

Cover bottom of greased pan with thin slices of apples.

Pour batter over apples and bake at 350° for about 45 minutes.

Makes a cake 8 x 10 x 1¼ inches.


Variation:

Use a deep loaf pan.

Melt 2 tablespoons butter in pan and add ¼ cup cane syrup.

Add 1 cup seedless raisins.

Cover with 1 cup thinly sliced apples.

Cook gently on top of stove or in oven for 15 minutes.

Add gingerbread batter and bake at 350° for 40 minutes.

# Raw Apple Cake

½ cup shortening
1 cup sugar
2 cups cake flour
2 eggs
½ teaspoon salt
1½ teaspoons soda

1 teaspoon cinnamon
1½ cups finely chopped apples
(tart ones)
1 cup chopped raisins
1 cup chopped nuts

Sift flour; measure and add sugar, soda, salt and cinnamon. Sift again. Work the shortening into this mixture as for pastry. Add beaten eggs. Stir in chopped nuts and raisins that have been dusted with flour. Add chopped apples and stir only enough to blend ingredients together. Pour into a greased loaf pan.
Bake at 325° for 1 hour. Makes a loaf 4 x 8 x 3½ inches.
If apples are not tart, use only 1 teaspoon soda.

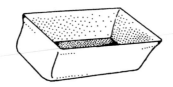

# Dried Apple Cake

1 cup dried apples
1 cup dark syrup
1 egg
¾ cup sour cream
1 cup sugar

1¾ cups all-purpose flour
1 teaspoon baking soda
1 teaspoon cinnamon
½ teaspoon cloves
½ teaspoon salt

Soak dried apples overnight.
In the morning chop in small pieces and cook slowly in the syrup for 45 minutes.
While apples cool, pour sour cream into a bowl.
Add egg and beat thoroughly.
Add sugar and continue to beat.
Sift flour; measure and add salt, soda, and cloves. Sift again.
Add sifted dry ingredients to mixture.
Beat thoroughly and then add apples. Blend together.
Pour into a greased loaf pan 5 x 9 x 4 inches.
Bake at 325° for 1 hour.

# Other
# Desserts

# Apple Dumplings

1½ C. sugar
1½ C. water
¼ tsp. cinnamon
½ tsp. nutmeg
3 T. butter or oleo
6 medium (any good) cooking apples

2 C. flour
2 tsp. baking powder
1 tsp. salt
⅔ C. shortening
½ C. milk

Combine sugar, water, spices. Bring to a boil; add butter. Sift together dry ingredients and cut in shortening. Add milk all at once and stir until flour is just moistened. Roll 1/8-inch thick on a floured surface. Cut with a knife into squares. Place the apple halves together after putting a pinch of butter, sugar, nutmeg and cinnamon where the core was. Then wrap the dough firmly around apple. (I use both hads to press it around.) Place apples about 1-inch apart in a baking dish. Prick the top with sunburst pattern and pour the syrup over the apples. Have the oven hot before you put them in because the syrup causes them to soften up too much and come apart. Heat oven to 375° about 35 minutes.

# Apple Brownies

1 stick margarine
1 C. brown sugar
2 eggs
1 tsp. vanilla
¼ tsp. ginger
¼ tsp. cinnamon

¼ tsp. nutmeg
¾ C. flour
1 tsp. baking powder
¼ tsp. salt
1 large and 2 small apples
   (chopped)

Cream margarine and sugar. Add eggs, vanilla, and spices. Beat until fluffy. Mix flour, baking powder, and salt. Add to first ingredients and beat until fluffy. Pour into greased 9x9-inch baking dish. Top with pecans. Bake at 325° for 30 minutes. Cool and cut into squares.

# Apple Bars

2 C. flour
½ C. sugar
½ tsp. baking powder
½ tsp. salt
1 C. margarine

4 medium apples (sliced, 4 C.)
¼ C. flour
¾ C. sugar
1 tsp. cinnamon

Combine first 4 ingredients. Cut in margarine. Stir in 2 egg yolks. Divide mixture in half. Put half in bottom of a cookie sheet. Combine apples, flour, sugar, and cinnamon. Arrange over crust. Crumble remaining dough over apples. Brush 1 egg white over all. Bake at 350° for 40-45 minutes. Drizzle frosting over the top. Yield: 4 dozen.

# Apple Crisp Pudding

6 or 8 apples (sliced)
1 tsp. cinnamon
½ C. water

½ C. butter
1 C. sugar
¾ C. flour

Butter casserole and add apples, water and cinnamon. Work together sugar, flour and butter until crumbly; sprinkle over apple mixture. Bake, uncovered at 350° for 30 minutes.

# Honeyed Apple Rings

2 large apples
1 C. honey
¼ C. water

1 T. lemon juice
2 sticks cinnamon
4 whole cloves

Wash and core apples, cut crosswise into 4 slices each. Place in baking dish. Mix honey, water, vinegar, and spices. Pour over apples. Bake, uncovered in a moderate oven (375°) 30 to 40 minutes.

# Apple Oatmeal Pudding

3 C. sliced apples
½ C. sugar
1 T. flour
1/8 tsp. salt
1/8 tsp. cinnamon
½ C. brown sugar

½ C. flour
½ C. raw oatmeal
1/8 tsp. salt
1/8 tsp. baking powder
¼ C. butter

Combine sliced apples, sugar, flour, salt and cinnamon. Place in baking dish. Crumble with fingers the brown sugar, flour, oatmeal, salt, baking powder and butter. Put on top of first layer and bake at 350° for 30-40 minutes or until apples are tender.

# Chewy Apple Cobbler

6 C. thinly sliced apples
½ C. uncooked rolled oats
½ C. frozen apple juice concentrate
   (thawed but undiluted)

1 tsp. cinnamon
¼ tsp. cloves
2 T. raisins
⅓ C. crunchy cereal
   (such as Grape Nuts)

Layer the oats in the bottom of an 8-inch square non-stick pan or pan sprayed with non-stick vegetable spray. Add the apple slices. Combine the apple juice concentrate, cinnamon, and cloves; pour over the apples and oats. Sprinkle with raisins on top. Cover with foil and bake at 350° for 1 hour. Remove the foil. Cover the top of the apples with crunchy cereal and bake an additional 10 minutes.

# Apple Dumplings

SYRUP:
2 C. sugar
2 C. water
¼ tsp. cinnamon

¼ tsp. nutmeg
¼ C. butter or margarine

DOUGH:
2 C. flour
1 tsp. salt
2 tsp. baking powder

¾ C. shortening
½ C. milk

Make syrup of sugar, water, cinnamon and nutmeg; add butter. Pare and core apples, cut into fourths. Sift flour, salt and baking powder. Cut in shortening. Add milk all at once and stir until moistened. Roll ¼-inch thick, cut into 5-inch squares. Arrange 4 pieces of apple on each square, sprinkle generously with additional sugar, cinnamon and nutmeg, dot with butter. Fold corners to center, pinch edges together. Place 1-inch apart in greased baking pan about 9 × 13-inch pan. Pour syrup over them. Bake in moderate oven 375°, about 35 minutes. Makes 8 dumplings.

# Apple Pudding

1 egg
¾ C. sugar
2 T. flour
1¼ tsp. baking powder

1/8 tsp. salt
1 C. chopped nuts
½ C. chopped apples
1 tsp. vanilla

Beat egg and sugar together until smooth, combine flour, baking powder, salt; stir into egg mixture. Add nuts, apples and vanilla. Bake in a greased pie pan in moderate oven (325°) for 30 minutes. Serve with whipped cream or ice cream.

# Apple Crisp

6 apples (sliced)
1 C. sugar
1 T. cinnamon

2 C. brown sugar
1 C. flour
¼ C. butter

Mix apples, sugar and cinnamon; put in bottom of pie pan. Mix brown sugar, flour and butter. Put on top. Bake at 350° for 30-35 minutes. Let cool. Serve with whipped cream.

# Apple Oat Crisp

**FRUIT:**
3 sm. apples, cored &
   sliced
1/2 c. applesauce

1 1/2 tsp. lemon juice
1/2 tsp. lemon rind, grated
1 tsp. sugar
1/4 tsp. cinnamon

**TOPPING:**
1/3 c. oatmeal, dry
2 T. wholewheat flour
2 T. brown sugar, firmly
   packed

1/4 tsp. cinnamon
1 T. plus 1 tsp. diet
   margarine

1. In a medium non-aluminum bowl, combine all fruit ingredients; pour into an 8-inch square baking dish.
2. Prepare topping in a small bowl by combining oatmeal, flour, brown sugar and cinnamon.
3. Cut margarine into topping mixture with a pastry blender until crumbly.
4. Sprinkle topping evenly over apple mixture.
5. Bake at 350°F. for 35 to 40 minutes until apples are tender and topping is browned; serve hot.

**Yield: 4 servings**

# More Apple Crisp

4 or 5 C. sliced apples
1 T. flour

½ C. sugar

TOPPING:
¾ C. brown sugar
⅓ C. butter
½ C. oatmeal
¾ C. flour

¼ tsp. soda
½ tsp. salt
1 tsp. cinnamon

Mix apples, flour and sugar together; place in an 8 x 8-inch baking dish. Mix together brown sugar, butter, flour, oatmeal, soda, salt and cinnamon and sprinkle over the apple mixture. Bake at 350° for 30 minutes or microwave on high setting for 16-18 minutes.

# Apple Pastry Squares

2¾ C. all-purpose flour
¾ C. butter or margarine
1 large egg
¼ C. milk
8 med. size apples

½ C. sugar
1 tsp. cinnamon

1 C. cereal flakes
Milk

FROSTING:
1 C. powdered sugar
1 tsp. vanilla
2 T. water

Cut flour and butter with pastry blender; beat egg and ¼ C. milk together and mix with flour mixture to form firm dough. Divide and refrigerate. Preheat oven to 400°. Grease and flour 15½-inch jelly roll pan. Peel, core and slice apples; mix with ½ C. sugar and cinnamon. Roll dough and put in pan. Sprinkle with cereal flakes. Spoon apple mixture on top, then roll and place dough on top for top crust. Brush top with milk. Bake 1 hour at 400°. Cool. Drizzle confectioners frosting on top of warm pie and cut in squares.

# Easy Apple Crisp

½ C. butter
½ C. brown sugar
½ C. white sugar
¾ C. flour

4 C. diced apples
2 T. water
2 tsp. cinnamon
½ C. oatmeal

Mix cinnamon, butter, sugars, flour, and oatmeal. Pour over apples in 8x8-inch pan. Bake at 350° for 1 hour. Can easily double this recipe and use double ingredients and 9x13-inch pan.

# Apple Pastry Squares

1½ C. sugar
1 tsp. cinnamon
½ tsp. nutmeg
8 C. sliced apples
  (7 large or 3 lbs.)
1½ tsp. salt

4 C. all-purpose flour
1½ C. shortening
2 beaten eggs
¼ C. lemon juice
2 T. butter or margarine

POWDERED SUGAR ICING:
1 C. powdered sugar

2 T. milk

In an extra large bowl, combine sugar, cinnamon, and nutmeg; add apple slices and toss to coat. Meanwhile, in another extra large bowl, stir together the all-purpose flour and 1½ tsp. salt with a pastry blender. Cut in the shortening until pieces are the size of small peas. In a small bowl, combine eggs, 6 T. water, and lemon juice. Add to flour mixture and mix until flour mixture is moistened. Divide the dough in half. On a lightly floured surface, roll half of the pastry to a 16x11-inch rectangle. Ease pastry into a 15x10x1-inch jelly roll pan (should be a ½-inch pastry border around the pan). Arrange apple slices evenly over the pastry in pan. Dot with butter. Roll out remaining dough to a 15½x10½-inch rectangle. Fit dough over apples. Seal and crimp pastry edges together. Cut several slits on top. Bake at 375° for 40 to 45 minutes or until crust is golden. Drizzle powdered sugar icing over hot pastry. To serve, cut pastry into squares. Makes 12 to 16 servings.

# Apple Crisp

2 C. brown sugar
1 C. flour
½ C. oleo or butter (cold)

3-4 C. apples (chopped)
1 tsp. cinnamon
½ C. sugar

Mix brown sugar, flour and shortening until crumbly. Spread ½ apples in 8x8 or 9x9-inch pan. Sprinkle ½ of sugar and cinnamon over apples. Add ½ of crumb mixture. Repeat layers. Bake at 350° for 45 minutes.

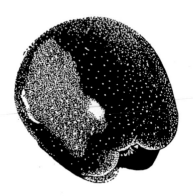

# Apple Squares

1 (18½ oz.) pkg. yellow pudding
  cake mix
½ C. soft butter
¼ C. brown sugar

½ tsp. cinnamon
3 large Red Delicious apples
1 C. sour cream
1 egg

Combine cake mix and butter; mix until crumbly. Reserve ⅔ C. for topping; add brown sugar and cinnamon to this reserved topping. Mix well and set aside. Press remaining cake batter mixture into bottom of ungreased 9x13-inch pan. Arrange apple slices over base. Blend sour cream and egg; spread evenly over apples. Sprinkle reserved topping mixture over all. Bake at 350° for 25 to 30 minutes or until topping is golden brown and bubbly. Serve warm. Refrigerate leftovers. Yields: 12 to 15 squares.

# Applesauce Bread Pudding

8 slices day old white bread
16 oz. can applesauce or 2 C.
½ tsp. cinnamon
½ C. brown sugar
2 eggs

2½ C. milk
½ tsp. vanilla
¼ tsp. salt
Margarine

Spread one side of each slice of bread with margarine. If desired, remove crusts. Arrange 4 slices of bread, buttered side up, in a greased 8x8-inch square pan or baking dish. Mix together applesauce, cinnamon, and 2 T. of brown sugar. Spread over bread in dish. Cut each remaining slice of bread into four triangles and arrange on filling in baking dish covering entire surface. Beat together eggs, milk, vanilla, salt, and remaining brown sugar. Pour over bread and sprinkle with additional cinnamon. Bake at 350° or 325° for glass for 50 to 55 minutes. Can be served with milk, ice cream or whipped topping.

# Apple Cobbler

5 C. apples
1 C. sugar
1½ C. all-purpose flour
1 T. sugar
2 tsp. baking powder

½ tsp. salt
⅓ C. shortening
½ C. milk
½ tsp. cinnamon

Spread sliced apples in a 9x9-inch baking dish. Mix together 1 C. sugar and cinnamon; spread over sliced apples. Put in 400° oven for 10 minutes. Mix together flour, 1 T. sugar, baking powder, and salt. Cut in shortening. Beat egg, add milk to egg and add to dry ingredients. Drop over hot apples and sprinkle 1 T. sugar over batter. Bake at 400° for 25 minutes.

# Fruit Crisp

1 (21 oz.) can apple, blueberry, cherry or peach pie filling
1 tsp. lemon juice
⅓ C. Gold Medal all-purpose flour

¼ C. brown sugar (packed)
½ tsp. ground cinnamon
3 T. margarine or butter
1 C. bran cereal (slightly crushed)*

Heat oven to 350°. Grease square pan, 8x8x2 or 9x9x2-inches. Mix pie filling and lemon juice. Spread in pan. Mix flour, brown sugar and cinnamon; cut in margarine until mixture is crumbly. Stir in cereal. Sprinkle over pie filling. Bake 15 to 20 minutes or until filling is hot and bubbly. Serve with vanilla ice cream if desired. Makes 6 servings. (*Place cereal between waxed paper, plastic wrap or in plastic bag; crush with rolling pin. Or crush in blender or food processor.)

# Apple Kuchen

½ C. flour
¾ C. brown sugar
½ C. rolled oats
¾ tsp. cinnamon

¾ tsp. nutmeg
⅓ C. butter or margarine
4-6 C. apples
1 tsp. lemon juice

Mix shortening with dry ingredients until crumbly for topping. Peel, core and slice apples in 8 or 9-inch square pan with lemon juice. Sprinkle oat crumble over. Bake at 350° for 30 to 35 minutes or until golden brown and apples pierced with a fork are tender.

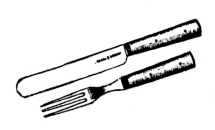

# Apple Cranberry Dumpling

SYRUP:

2 C. water

2 C. sugar

½ tsp. cloves

½ C. butter

BISCUIT DOUGH:

2 C. flour (sifted)

1 T. baking powder

1 tsp. salt

2 T. sugar

½ C. shortening

¾ C. milk

FILLING:

4 C. apples (grated or thin sliced)

½ C. black walnuts (chopped)

1 C. whole cranberries (drained, cooked) or canned whole sauce

Combine first 4 ingredients for syrup; boil 5 minutes. Remove and add butter. Sift dry ingredients and cut in shortening. Add milk, tossing to make soft dough. Roll to 18x12-inch. Spread with apples, cranberries and nuts. Roll like jelly roll. Slice 1-inch slices and place in 9x13-inch pan. Pour over hot syrup. Bake at 425° for 40 minutes. Serve warm. Makes 12 servings.

# Fruit Cobbler

½ C. oleo

¾ C. white flour

¼ tsp. salt

½ tsp. baking powder

½ tsp. cinnamon

¾ C. milk

¼ tsp. almond extract

1 (16 oz.) pkg. frozen fruit or 2-3 C. fresh fruit (sliced)

Melt butter in an 8-inch square baking dish. Combine flour and next 5 ingredients; pour over butter. Do not stir. Arrange fruit on top. Bake at 350°

# Apple Cranberry Bake

3 C. tart diced apples (peeled)
2 C. fresh whole cranberries
¼ C. white sugar
¼ C. brown sugar

1½ C. rolled oats
⅓ C. flour
⅓ C. oleo (melted)

Mix apples, cranberries and sugar in 10x13-inch pan. In bowl, melt oleo; add other topping ingredients. Sprinkle over fruit. Bake 55 to 60 minutes at 350°.

# Apple-Cherry Crisp

1 can (21 ounces) cherry pie filling
1 medium baking apple, peeled,
   cored and thinly sliced
2 teaspoons slivered lemon peel
½ cup packed brown sugar
½ cup quick-cooking oats,
   uncooked

¼ cup all-purpose flour
¼ teaspoon ground cinnamon
3 tablespoons butter or margarine
Sweetened whipped cream or
   vanilla ice cream (optional)

1. Lightly grease 10- by 6-inch baking dish. In medium bowl, combine pie filling, apple and peel. Spoon into dish.

2. To make topping: In small bowl, combine sugar, oats, flour and cinnamon. With pastry blender or fork, cut in butter until mixture resembles coarse crumbs; sprinkle over filling mixture. Bake, uncovered, at 375°F. 25 minutes or until golden brown. Spoon warm crisp into dessert dishes; top with whipped cream or ice cream, if desired. Makes 6 to 8 servings.

# Apple Betty

4 C. tart apples (sliced & pared)
¼ C. orange juice
1 C. sugar
¾ C. all-purpose flour (sifted)

½ tsp. ground cinnamon
¼ tsp. ground nutmeg
Dash of salt
½ C. butter

Mound apples in buttered 9-inch pie plate; sprinkle with orange juice. Combine sugar, flour, spices and salt. Cut in butter until mixture is crumbly. Sprinkle over apples. Bake at 375° for 45 minutes or until apples are tender and topping is crisp. Serve warm with cream. Makes 6 servings.

# Applesauce Brownies

1 oz. unsweetened chocolate
1 C. cake flour (sifted)
¼ C. cocoa powder
½ tsp. salt
3 large egg whites

2 large eggs
1¼ C. sugar
¼ C. corn syrup
1 C. applesauce
1 T. vanilla extract

Preheat oven to 350°. Melt chocolate in a small pan or bowl over hot water or in microwave on ½ power (defrost). Set aside. In a medium sized bowl, add flour, cocoa and salt. Stir. In a large bowl, whisk egg whites and whole eggs. Add sugar, corn starch, applesauce and vanilla. Then whisk in chocolate. Add flour mixture to the egg mixture and blend well. Grease a 9x13-inch baking pan with non-stick spray. Pour in batter and bake for 30 minutes or until an inserted toothpick comes out clean. Cool in the pan on a rack. Cut into 24 squares. (85 calories)

# Apple Dumplings

6 tart apples such as Jonathan, Golden Delicious, Lura Red or Rome Beauty (peeled & cored)

PASTRY:
2¼ C. flour                          2 tsp. baking powder
¾ C. Crisco                          1 tsp. salt
7-8 T. ice water

FILLING:
⅔ C. sugar                           Raisins (optional)
1½ tsp. cinnamon

SAUCE:
2 C. sugar                           ¼ tsp. nutmeg
2 C. water                           2-3 T. butter
½ tsp. cinnamon

For Filling: Mix and set aside.

For Sauce: Bring all but butter to a boil; add butter and set aside.

For Pastry: Prepare pastry as for pie dough; shape into ball. Roll out and cut into 6 (5-inch) squares. Place apple in center of each pastry square. Fill hole with 1 T. of filling and 1 tsp. butter. Fold up corners of dough over apple. Pinch edges closed. (A few drops of water if needed to make dough stick together.) Place in oiled glass pan; refrigerate at least 2 hours. Pour prepared sauce over apples; bake 12 minutes at 500°, then 45 minutes at 350°. Serve warm with whipped cream or ice cream.

# Dumplings For Apples, Rhubarb, or Raspberries

SAUCE:

1½ C. sugar (scant)
1 T. all-purpose flour
½ tsp. ground cinnamon
¼ tsp. salt

1½ C. water
⅓ C. butter or margarine
1 tsp. vanilla extract
Red food coloring (optional)

DOUGH:

2 C. all-purpose flour
2 T. sugar
2 tsp. baking powder

¼ tsp. salt
2½ T. cold butter or margarine
¾ C. milk

FILLING:

2 T. butter or margarine
   (softened)
½ C. sugar
½ tsp. ground cinnamon

2 C. fresh or frozen apples,
   rhubarb or raspberries (finely
   chopped

For Sauce: In a saucepan, combine sugar, flour, cinnamon and salt. Stir in water; add butter. Bring to a boil; cook and stir 1 minute. Remove from heat. Add vanilla and, if desired, enough food coloring to tint sauce a deep pink; set aside.

For Dough: In a medium bowl, combine flour, suar, baking powder and salt. Cut in butter until mixture resembles coarse crumbs. Add milk and mix quickly. Do not overmix. Gather dough into a ball and roll out on a floured surface into a 12x9-inch rectangle. Spread with softened butter; arrange rhubarb on top. Combine sugar and cinnamon; sprinkle over rhubarb. Roll up from the long side and place on a cutting board, seam side down. Cut roll into 12 slices. Arrange slices, cut side up, in a greased 9x13x2-inch baking dish. Pour sauce over. Bake at 350° for 35 to 40 minutes or until golden brown. Yield: 12 servings.

# Cheese Apple Crisp For A Bunch

3½ qts. apples (peeled & thinly sliced)
1½ tsp. cinnamon
3½ C. sugar
¾ C. water
1½ T. lemon juice

2 C. flour (sifted)
¾ tsp. salt
½ lb. butter
1 (12 oz.) grated cheese (aged Cheddar or process American)

Put apples in large shallow baking pan; add cinnamon, little sugar, water and lemon juice. In mixing bowl, combine remaining sugar, flour and salt. Work in butter to form crumbly mixture. Lightly stir in grated cheese and spread mixture over apples. Bake at 350° for 30 to 35 minutes. Cut in squares. (Double everything for 40.)

# Microwave Apple Crisp

6 C. apples (cored, peeled & sliced)
¼ C. sugar
1 T. all-purpose flour
½ tsp. ground cinnamon
1 C. quick-cooking rolled oats
¼ C. brown sugar (packed)

1 tsp. ground cinnamon
1/8 tsp. ground nutmeg
½ C. butter or margarine (softened)
¼ C. coconut
¼ C. pecans or almonds (chopped)

In an 8x8x2-inch dish, place apples. In small bowl, combine ¼ C. sugar 1 T. flour and ½ tsp. cinnamon. Toss with apples to coat. In large mixing bowl, combine remaining flour, brown sugar, 1 tsp. cinnamon and nutmeg. Cut in softened butter or margarine until mixture is crumbly. Stir in coconut and nuts. Sprinkle topping over apples. Microwave on High (100%) for 1: to 14 minutes or until apples are tender. Makes 6 to 8 servings.

# Applesauce Or Rhubarb Bars

1 tsp. soda
1 C. sugar
¼ C. brown sugar
1½ sticks oleo
1 tsp. vanilla
2 C. flour

1 C. applesauce or cooked
  rhubarb
Nuts & Raisins (optional)
½ C. sugar
1 tsp. cinnamon

Mix all ingredients except sugar and cinnamon. Spread in jelly roll pan; sprinkle with sugar and cinnamon and chopped nuts if desired. Bake 30 minutes at 350°

# Apple Crisp

3 c. sliced apples
1 c. sugar
1 T. flour
⅛ tsp. salt
1 tsp. cinnamon
¼ tsp. soda

¼ tsp. baking powder
⅓ c. melted butter
¾ c. rolled oats (oatmeal)
¾ c. flour
¾ c. brown sugar

Mix apples, sugar, 1 tablespoon flour, salt and cinnamon in baking dish. Combine remaining ingredients and crumble over apples. Bake in slow to moderate oven (325° to 350°) for 45 minutes. If too dry, add a little water.

# Baked Tapioca Pudding

2 C. apples (sliced)
2 C. boiling water
½ C. brown or white sugar
¼ C. tapioca

¼ tsp. salt
½ tsp. cinnamon
2 T. butter
Vanilla

Put apples in baking dish; pour water and sugar over. Bake 15 minutes in 400° oven. Mix tapioca, salt, cinnamon and vanilla. Stir into apples. Bake 15 minutes or until done.

# Applesauce Molasses Bars

1 C. butter
½ C. brown sugar (firmly packed)
1 C. sugar
½ C. molasses
2 eggs
1 C. applesauce
3 C. flour (sifted)
2 tsp. baking powder
½ tsp. baking soda
½ tsp. salt
½ tsp. ground cinnamon
½ C. dairy sour cream
1 (3 oz.) pkg. cream cheese (softened)
¼ C. butter (softened)
1⅔ C. confectioners sugar (sifted)
1 T. cream or milk
1 tsp. vanilla

Cream together butter, sugars and molasses. Add eggs, one at a time; beat well. Add applesauce. Sift together flour, baking powder, baking soda, salt and cinnamon. Add alternately with sour cream; mix well. Spread in greased 15½x10½x1-inch jelly roll pan. Bake in 350° oven 25 to 30 minutes or until done. When cool, frost with a cream cheese frosting. Blend together cheese and butter. Add confectioners sugar, cream and vanilla. Beat mixture until smooth. Makes about 3 dozen bars.

# Applesauce Turnovers

2 to 3 apples, peeled, cored & chopped; use a combination of Granny Smith & Jonagold or Golden Delicious
1/2 to 2/3 c. sugar, to taste & tartness of apples
1 T. lemon juice (opt.)
1 tsp. cinnamon
1 T. cornstarch

Heat oven to 400°. Mix chopped apples with the rest of ingredients in small saucepan. Cook over medium heat just until apples begin to be tender and mixture thickens. Remove from heat.

Roll out pie crust to 1/8-inch thickness. Use 3- to 4-inch round cookie cutters to cut out rounds of dough. If you don't have cutter this size, use small saucer and cut around it to form circle. Place dough on ungreased cookie sheet and put small amount of apple mixture in middle of crust (1/2 to 1 teaspoon). Fold crust over to form half circle. Crimp edges with a fork and make small slit in top to vent. Mix 2 teaspoons of sugar to 1/4 teaspoon of cinnamon. Sprinkle additional cinnamon and sugar over tops of turnovers.

# Miscellaneous

# Apple and Wild Rice Dressing

½ C. chopped onion
2 T. vegetable oil
1 C. ea. white & wild rice (rinse & drain*)
4 C. hot water
¾ tsp. salt
½ tsp. each thyme & oregano (crushed)
¼ tsp. pepper
3 C. (about 1 lb.) cored & chopped
   Golden Delicious apples
½ C. coarsely chopped pecans
   or hazel nuts
¼ C. chopped parsley

Sauté onion in oil until tender. Add white and wild rice; cook and stir until coated with oil. Add water, salt, thyme, oregano, and pepper; bring to a boil. Reduce heat, simmer, covered for 30 minutes. Add apples, nuts, and parsley. Continue to simmer or bake in 3-quart covered baking dish at 375° for 15 to 30 minutes or until liquid is absorbed and wild rice is tender. Makes 8 to 9 cups or enough stuffing for 12-pound turkey.

# Apple Bread

½ C. butter
1 C. sugar
2 eggs
1 tsp. vanilla
1 tsp. soda

½ tsp. salt
2 T. sour milk
2 C. diced apples
2 C. flour

TOPPING:
2 T. flour
2 T. sugar

1 tsp. cinnamon
2 T. melted butter

Cream together butter, sugar, eggs, vanilla and salt. Dissolve soda in sour milk, then add apples and flour. Add nuts, if desired. Put in 2 small or 1 large greased and floured loaf pan, then mix together butter, flour, sugar and cinnamon. Sprinkle on top of batter. Bake at 325° for 1 hour.

# Apple Butter

2 C. unsweetened applesauce
½ C. sugar
1 tsp. cinnamon

¼ tsp. allspice
1/8 tsp. ginger
1/8 tsp. cloves

Combine ingredients in a heavy 1½-quart saucepan. Bring to a boil and cook for 30 minutes. Makes 1¼ cups.

# Apple Cinnamon Jelly

7 C. apple juice
1 C. red cinnamon candies
8 C. sugar

1 box Sure-Jell fruit pectin
½ tsp. margarine or butter

Wash 6 lbs. or about 20 medium tart apples; core and slice into eighths. Add 6 C. water; bring to a boil and simmer 10 minutes covered. Stir occasionally, crushing fruit. Simmer 5 minutes more. Place hot sauce in a wet jelly bag or several thicknesses of cheesecloth or pillow case. Hang and allow to drip several hours; do not squeeze. Measure exact amount of juice and candies in large saucepan. Prepare jars and lids as directed on package. Measure sugar in separate bowl; stir fruit pectin into juice; add margarine. Bring to rolling boil, stirring constantly. Quickly stir in all sugar. Return to rolling boil and boil exactly 1 minute, stirring constantly. Remove from heat. Skim off any foam with metal spoon. Ladle quickly into prepared hot jars to within 1/8 inch of top. Wipe jar rims and threads. Cover with lid and screw tightly. Invert until cool. Fills about 11 (8 oz.) jars.

# Peanut Butter Fudge

| | |
|---|---|
| 2/3 c. nonfat dry powdered milk | 2 T. plus 2 tsp. frozen unsweetened concentrated apple juice, thawed |
| 1/4 c. chunky style peanut butter | |
| 1/4 c. raisins, chopped | 3/4 c. Rice Krispies |

1. In a small bowl, combine powdered milk with peanut butter, blending thoroughly; stir in raisins and apple juice.
2. Add cereal and stir until combined.
3. Press mixture into an 8 x 3 1/2 x 2 1/2-inch nonstick loaf pan.
4. Refrigerate until firm, about 2 hours.
5. To serve, cut into 8 squares; store in refrigerator.

**Yield: 8 squares**

# Mushroom Apple Stuffing

| | |
|---|---|
| 1/2 c. onion, minced | 1 tsp. nutmeg |
| 2 tsp. chicken bouillon granules | 1 tsp. sage |
| 8 oz. fresh mushrooms | 1 tsp. pepper |
| 2 T. Butter Buds | 1 tsp. curry |
| 1 c. water | 1/4 c. parsley |
| 4 med. green apples, chopped | 4 slices bread, toasted & cubed |
| 1 tsp. cinnamon | 1 c. water |

1. Brown first 5 ingredients in a nonstick skillet.
2. Add next 9 ingredients and simmer until apples are tender.
3. Place dressing in an 8-inch square casserole dish.
4. Cover and bake at 350°F. for 30 to 40 minutes.

**Yield: 4 servings**

# Apple Jelly

3 lbs. tart apples          2 T. lemon juice
3 C. water                3 C. sugar

Choose tart apples, ¾ of them fully ripe and ¼ under-ripe. Wash, remove stem and blossom ends. Do not peel or core. Cut apples into small pieces. Place apples and water in saucepan. Cover and bring to a boil over high heat. Reduce heat and simmer 20 to 25 minutes or until apples are soft. Place fruit in colander lined with cheesecloth or dampened jelly bag. Let fruit drip through without pressing so jelly will be clear. However, you will get more juice by pressing and/or twisting bag or using a fruit press. Measure apple juice into kettle. Add lemon juice and sugar; stir well. Bring to a boil over high heat until temperature is 120° or jelly mixture sheets from spoon. Remove from heat. Skim off foam quickly. Pour jelly immediately into hot, sterilized jars. Cover with 1/8-inch melted paraffin. Makes about 5 (6 oz.) jars.

VARIATION:
Crabapple Jelly - Use 3 lbs. crabapples and 3 C. water to make 4 C. juice. Omit lemon juice. Follow directions for making Apple Jelly.

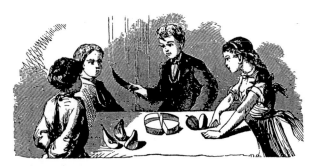

# Lo-Cal Apple Cinnamon Jelly

6 C. apple juice           1 box Sure-Jell (lower sugar)
½ C. red cinnamon candies    ½ tsp. margarine
4 C. sugar

Follow procesure as for regular jelly.

# Onion Apple Stuffing

½ C. sweet butter or margarine
18 med.-size onions (sliced)
5 celery ribs (sliced)
½ C. sweet butter
4 C. bread cubes (8 slices of
   bread, or more)

¼ C. fresh parsley (chopped)
1 T. fresh sage (chopped)
1 T. fresh thyme
½ tsp. freshly ground black
   pepper
4 large apples

In a large skillet, melt ½ C. butter. Add the onions and slowly cook for 3 hours. Add more butter if necessary. In a second skillet, melt another ½ C. butter and saute' the celery for 5 minutes. Toss in the bread cubes, herbs and black pepper. Peel, core and dice the apples. Mix with the other ingredients. When the onions are a rich brown, stir into the stuffing. Stuff into two 6 to 8 lb. geese or one 12 to 14 lb. turkey. Excess stuffing can be baked separately in a 1½ qt. greased baking dish for 45 minutes at 350°.


# Cherry Apple Jam

1 (16 oz.) pkg. pitted tart red
   cherries (frozen unsweetened)
1 med. apple (cored & finely
   chopped) 1 C.

¼ C. lemon juice
1 (1¾ oz.) pkg. regular powdered
   fruit pectin
5 C. sugar

Finely chop frozen cherries, reserving juices. You should have 3 C. chopped fruit. In an 8 or 10-qt. kettle or Dutch oven, combine chopped cherries, reserved juices, apple and lemon juice. Add pectin; mix well. Bring mixture to a full rolling boil. Stir in sugar. Bring again to full rolling boil, stirring often. Boil hard, uncovered, 1 minute. Remove from heat; quickly skim off foam with a metal spoon. Ladle into hot clean half-pint jars, leaving a ¼-inch headspace. Wipe jar rims; adjust lids. Process in boiling water bath for 15 minutes (start this timing when the water boils). Makes about 5 half-pints.

# Lo-Cal Apple Jam

5 C. prepared fruit
½ C. raisins
½ C. water
2 T. lemon juice (fresh best)
1 tsp. cinnamon

¼ tsp. allspice
3½ C. sugar
1 C. brown sugar
1 box Sure-Jell for lower sugar
½ tsp. margarine

Follow procedure as for regular jam.

# Dutch Apple Pie Jam

4 C. prepared tart apples
½ C. raisins
1¼ C. water
2 T. lemon juice (fresh best)
1 tsp. cinnamon

¼ tsp. allspice
4 C. sugar
1 C. brown sugar
1 box Sure-Jell
½ tsp. margarine or butter

Peel, core, chop finely. Add raisins and water into large saucepan. Add lemon juice and spices. Measure sugar into separate bowl. Add Sure-Jell into fruit; add margarine. Bring to boil on high, stirring constantly. Quickly stir in both sugars; return to boil and boil exactly 1 minute, stirring constantly. Remove from heat, skim off any foam with metal spoon. Ladle into hot prepared jars; seal as directed on Sure-Jell package.

# Apple Butter In Crock-Pot

12-14 cooking apples (to equal
8 C., chopped)
2 C. cider

2 C. sugar
1 tsp. ground cinnamon
¼ tsp. ground cloves

Core and chop apples. (Don't peel.) Combine apples and cider in crock pot. Cover and cook on low for 10 to 12 hours or until apples are mushy. Puree in food mill or sieve. Return mixture to pot; add sugar and spices. Cover and cook on low for 1 hour. Pour into sterilized jars and seal or pour into freezer containers and freeze. Makes about 8 C.

# Oven Apple Butter

10 lbs. tart apples (20-30 Jonathans or other)
3-5 C. sugar
4 sticks cinnamon (or ½ tsp. oil of cinnamon)
½ gal. of cider (boil down to ⅔ of amount)

1 thinly sliced lemon (or 1 T. lemon juice)
1 thinly sliced orange or orange juice (optional)
½ tsp. salt
1 tsp. vanilla

Peel, core and cook apples in roaster with reduced cider in low oven 250°-300°; 4 to 6 hours, stir occasionally. Add sugar and citrus slices (or juice) last hour of baking; add salt and vanilla. Remove cinnamon sticks and citrus slices before packing in hot, steril canning jars; seal.

# Apple Raisin Stuffing

½ C. minced onions
2 C. apples (diced)
4-6 C. bread cubes
½ tsp. salt

½ oleo (melted)
½ C. raisins
1 T. poultry seasoning
2 T. honey

Mix and use to stuff 8 to 10 lb. turkey.

# Apple Stuffing

1 1/2 c. onions, chopped
1/2 c. celery, sliced
1 frozen chicken stock cube, for sautéing (see index)
3 c. whole wheat bread, cut in cubes; can use any kind of bread

1/2 tsp. ground sage
1/4 tsp. thyme
1/4 tsp. nutmeg
1/4 c. parsley, chopped fine
Dash of nutmeg
1/2 c. chicken stock
3 c. finely-chopped apples

Sauté onion and celery in stock for 5 minutes. Add bread and seasonings, tossing until bread is lightly browned. Add stock to bread mixture very gradually, tossing during addition. Add the apples, blending well. Put in a 1 1/2 quart baking dish that has been sprayed with vegetable oil and bake in a 350° oven for 20 minutes, or until apples are tender and dressing is nicely browned.
**Yield: 8 servings.**

# Apple Chutney

4 C. peeled apples (chopped)
½ C. water
3 C. sugar
¼ C. vinegar

1 tsp. ground cinnamon
¼ tsp. ground cloves
¼ tsp. salt

Place apples and water in 2 qt. saucepan. Bring to a boil. Cover and simmer 10 minutes or until apples are tender. Stir in sugar, vinegar, cinnamon and cloves. Simmer, uncovered, 50 minutes or until mixture thickens. Pour into hot, sterilized jars to within ½-inch from top. Adjust jar lids. Process to boiling water bath 10 minutes. Makes 4 half-pints.

# Apple Tomato Chutney

2 T. plus oil
½ C. onion (chopped)
2 garlic cloves (minced)
1 tsp. curry powder

1 lg. can stewed tomatoes
¼ C. raisins
2 C. red or yellow Delicious
    apples (chopped)

Saute' onion and garlic in hot oil. Add all but apples and bring to simmer. Stir in chopped apples; cook 15 to 20 minutes. Good served with meat dishes.

# Apple Cranberry Relish

1 (12 oz.) pkg. cranberries (fresh
    or frozen)
1 C. honey
½ C. water

½ C. orange juice
2 apples (cored & diced)
¼ C. orange peel (shredded)

Bring all ingredients to a boil over medium heat. Continue boiling for 10 minute, or until cranberries pop open. Serve warm or refrigerate until ready to use.

# Uncooked Apple Cranberry Relish

2 apples (firm)
1 orange
½ C. sugar
2 C. cranberries
1 small onion (peeled & cut)

2 T. lemon juice
¼ tsp. red pepper
¼ tsp. cloves
1 tsp. ginger
1 T. brandy

Core and dice apples; chop or process coarsely in food processor. Process orange peel (remove white pith) with sugar until finely chopped. Add apples, then cranberries. Add orange juice with remaining ingredients; cover and refrigerate. Good served with meat dishes.

# Apple Stuffing

¼ C. onions (chopped)
¼ C. celery (chopped)
2 T. margarine
4 C. dry bread cubes
1 C. unpeeled apples (diced)

½ tsp. poultry seasoning
½ tsp. dried sage
½ C. chicken broth
Fresh ground black pepper

Cook onions and celery in margarine for 5 minutes or until tender. Combine onions and celery with all other dry ingredients. Add broth, and toss lightly. Bake in covered casserole for 30 minutes at 325°. Yield: 6 servings.

## To Order Copies

Please send me _____ copies of ***Apple A Day
Cookbook*** at $9.95 each plus $3.00 for the first
book and $.50 for each additional copy for S/H.
(Make checks payable to Hearts 'n Tummies.)

Name _____

Street _____

City _____ State _____ Zip _____

**Hearts 'n Tummies Cookbook Co.**
**3544 Blakslee Street**
**Wever, IA   52658**
**1-800-571-2665**

------------------------------------------------------------

## To Order Copies

Please send me _____ copies of ***Apple A Day
Cookbook*** at $9.95 each plus $3.00 for the first
book and $.50 for each additional copy for S/H.
(Make checks payable to Hearts 'n Tummies.)

Name _____

Street _____

City _____ State _____ Zip _____

**Hearts 'n Tummies Cookbook Co.**
**3544 Blakslee Street**
**Wever, IA   52658**
**1-800-571-2665**